The Career Coach

The Career Coach

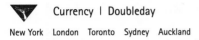

Winning Strategies for Getting Ahead in Today's Job Market

Gordon Miller

Currency | Doubleday

New York   London   Toronto   Sydney   Auckland

A CURRENCY BOOK
PUBLISHED BY DOUBLEDAY
a division of Random House, Inc.
1540 Broadway, New York, New York 10036

CURRENCY and DOUBLEDAY are
trademarks of Doubleday, a division
of Random House, Inc.

Book design by Richard Oriolo

LIBRARY OF CONGRESS CATALOGING-IN-PUBLICATION DATA

Miller, Gordon, 1948–
The career coach: winning strategies for getting ahead
in today's job market / Gordon Miller.—1st ed.
p. cm.
1. Career development.   I. Title.
HF5381 .M483 2001
650.14—dc21
00-047571

ISBN 0-385-49600-1

SPECIAL SALES
Currency Books are available at special discounts for
bulk purchases for sales promotions or premiums. Special editions, including personalized covers, excerpts of
existing books, and corporate imprints, can be created
in large quantities for special needs. For more information, write to Special Markets, Currency Books,
280 Park Avenue, 11th Floor, New York, NY 10017, or
e-mail specialmarkets@randomhouse.com.

1 3 5 7 9 10 8 6 4 2

To Deborah. You are a dream come true. I can't wait to spend the rest of my life with you.

To Brett and Kacey. I'm so proud of you. I adore you.

To Brandon and Ryan. You bring so much joy. You guys are awesome.

Acknowledgments

Special thanks to Paul Wyman for your great work in creating the "exercises" pages at the end of each chapter in this book. You are an excellent coach and very talented person.

Thanks to Jody Rein, my literary agent, for helping me find Doubleday. You are the best!

Thanks to Roger Scholl, Stephanie Land, and others at Doubleday for bringing this book to market. You have been terrific to work with!

Thanks to Marty Slattery, my writing coach. You are incredible!

To countless friends, colleagues, and family that have contributed to my support, thank you.

Contents

The Career Coach

Prologue

When smashing monuments, save the pedestals—
they always come in handy.
—STANISLAW LEC, *UNKEMPT THOUGHTS*

Don't you just hate prologues? Me, too. That's why this one is so brief. And it's actually just a disclaimer.

WARNING!!!
If you already have a job and are satisfied with it, think you are well compensated for your efforts, and have a clear career path to the top, don't bother to read on.

There. I've just eliminated the 1 percent of the workforce for whom *The Career Coach* doesn't apply. And even that 1 percent figure is probably overstated.

Instead of thanking the hundreds of people who helped me get this far in life, I'm just going to highlight a few things I'd like you to think about as you get into the book. Perhaps most important of all: **THE RULES HAVE CHANGED.** Companies don't operate the way they did ten (or even five) years ago. The idea that you were going to go to work for a company and stay there for thirty years is pretty much a thing of the past. Except in a few isolated cases, it just won't happen. It's not good or bad: It's just the way it is today.

As companies begin to flatten organization structures in order to respond quickly to ever-changing market pressures, there won't be much of a corporate ladder to climb anymore. More of us will be moving to the front lines, having more authority and making more decisions. There won't be that lofty, top-heavy management structure that we grew up with. We need to begin to think of ourselves as "change agents." What's a change agent? Someone who not only supports change, but actually proposes and endorses change on a regular basis.

Some of the changes will be radical; a few monuments might be smashed along the way, but as Mr. Lec suggests, we'll save the pedestals because they will, in fact, come in handy.

You are now officially welcomed to a forum of new and old ideas, of cherished opinions, some of which may even change before you're finished reading.

This book is a truly *interactive* work, taking advantage of the Internet to provide assistance and explanation beyond what you will find in these pages. Whenever you see a symbol like this ▷ you are invited to go to my Career Coaching Web site, http://www.deltaroad.com. On the home page of that site, simply click on the symbol, and you'll have at your fingertips access to on-line tutorials, assessments, quizzes, samples, examples, case studies, and in-depth information to help you work through the concepts and exercises in *The Career Coach*.

Good luck! Remember, in today's world, it's no longer a career "path," it's a high-speed road. We call it "the Delta Road."

—GORDON MILLER

What Is a Career Coach, Anyway?

*Opportunities multiply
as they are seized.*
—SUN TZU

career 1: a field, or pursuit of, progressive achievement esp. in public,
professional and business life . . . 2: a course or passage.
coach 1: an instructor or trainer 2: the person who is in charge of the
team and the strategy . . .

Melissa was not a happy camper when she first came to see me. She was working far too many hours, she wasn't all that crazy about her boss, and her career just didn't seem to be going anywhere. And (perhaps most important) she wasn't having any fun. She had a bad case of "Is this all there is?" and didn't know what to do about it. Fortunately, our paths crossed not long after that, and my extensive experience in the job market (not all good, by the way) allowed me to help her through a difficult time.

So what is a career coach? Simply put, it's someone who will help you plan, implement, and manage a successful and satisfying career strategy. Or, in some cases, just provide you with the information you need to get over the rough spots on the journey. But just as most folks don't go to the doctor until they're feeling poorly, most folks don't even think about going to someone who can help them with their career until the sky is falling and Chicken Little has already marched off to spread the word. Some people are smart enough to see a doctor for an annual checkup, thereby preventing the entire sky from falling; others wait until they feel the first patch of blue bounce off their head. The same cautionary message applies to consultation with a career coach—don't wait until the pink slip is in your final pay envelope, or until your "happy meter," as I call it, is dangerously close to zero before you seek assistance. *The Career Coach* is an effort to distill some of the decades of my experience and training into book form in order to help guide you on your career path.

I recommend that you periodically refer back to this book, as it can be an enormous plus in your job search or career advancement strategy. Just how beneficial it will be is largely up to you. Most of you are already familiar with the concept of a personal trainer: the person you go to when your tummy spills over the belt of your pants or your thighs and behind begin to jiggle like Jell-O, and you are driven out of complacency to finally decide to do something about it. The personal trainer should be well versed on all the research, know all the latest training techniques, and actually show you how to get rid of those unsightly bulges. Even if you know what it takes to get in better shape, you may, like so many of us, need that "mentor" to inspire and keep you motivated, to keep you focused on what's really going to help.

The Career Coach is to your work environment what the personal trainer is to your physical conditioning. Remember, there is no magic wand to wave, no magic pill that you can take to get a better job or inspire your career advancement opportunities. Those of you fighting the oblique muscle syndrome, commonly known as "love handles," know that wishing them away does no good. The only way to reduce or eliminate them requires a willingness to work and pinpointing the right direction toward accomplishing your goals.

How does *The Career Coach* work? While you're toiling away at your job, nose firmly affixed to the grindstone, just trying to survive or even get ahead a bit, I'm out surfing the job market, gathering information for this book, looking at future trends and new opportunities, exploring new industries and hot markets, making contact with the people and companies who can help your career flourish in the future.

Here are just some of the things I'm going to tell you, listed here in no particular order of importance:

1. How the nature of work is changing, and how to better position yourself to take advantage of these changes.

2. How to successfully change careers, or switch industries or fields altogether.

3. How to negotiate a big raise, or get a piece of the action, whether bonuses or stock options (it's easier than you think).

4. How to map out your career as part of a strategic plan.

5. How to become proactive rather than reactive, so you don't miss out on the great opportunities coming down the pike.

6. How to develop career-enhancing relationships with the people who can make a difference in helping you build a satisfying and well-paid career.

7. When and how to use the Internet to further your career goals.

8. How anyone can become a star performer, greatly enhancing his or her value to the company.

9. Why résumés are becoming a thing of the past, and how they rule you out instead of in. Effective steps you can take instead of flooding the market with tired chronological listings of past jobs.

10. Killer interviewing techniques. No, not the tired tips you've heard about dozens of times. I'm talking about new techniques for the new marketplace, the ones that will distinguish you from the parade of other applicants applying for the job.

And there is much, much more. So don't close this book, and don't close your eyes. As they say in the news business, film at eleven. Stay tuned.

I'm sure it will come as no surprise that I charge a hefty fee for my work with clients. Only a small portion of my heart or time is devoted to altruistic concerns (mostly reserved for immediate family). For my work with clients—who, by the way, are to a person extremely satisfied—I charge an average rate of three hundred fifty dollars an hour. Typically, I spend somewhere between ten and twenty hours working with each client. I've had clients whose consultation took less than ten hours, although none has taken more than twenty. That's a range of roughly thirty-five hundred to seven thousand dollars per client. A lot of money? Perhaps. But how much is a happy, prosperous career worth? Those of you smart enough to purchase *The Career Coach* can get much of the same advice and strategy I offer clients individually just by reading the information on the pages that follow (though you may need a session or two on the phone with one of our career coaches if your situation falls into the "very difficult" category).

I don't have a degree in career coaching. As far as I know, they don't *give* degrees in career coaching. My training was all OJT: On the Job Training, two decades as employee and divisional manager. I hired and fired and guided the careers of those under me. In my twenty-five years in the corporate structure, I worked with thousands of people, got to see firsthand what employees thought they needed to do to get ahead and what actually helped to advance their careers; what bosses said and did right, what they did wrong, and how that affected employee performance. I saw countless people who never reached their potential, who left companies over issues that were rectifiable.

And because I've had twenty-five years of learning those lessons, of hiring and directing and motivating people, I was able to put into practice much of what I had learned on the front lines of the job scene. When I was able to take off the hat that said "BOSS" (with all it implies), and become part of the team, my job became one of providing my clients with the tools for success. And *voilà!,* top performing teams started to develop.

Call it trial and error, call it trial by experience, call it anything you want, but just by being present for a lengthy period of time in the bubbling cauldron that is corporate America, I began to understand the company dynamics, the personal emotions, the politics involved, and the requirements necessary to be a top producer.

In my last ten years in the job market, my career began to rapidly outpace that of my peers. For various reasons I kept getting the quicker promotion, the bigger raises and bonuses, the better salary and benefits packages. Believe me, it wasn't because I was smarter or worked harder. People lots smarter than me are presently wallowing in the same corporate backwater where they have been treading water for the last fifteen years. They're not actually drowning, but they're not making it to shore either. They are usually clinging to an old weathered life preserver that says simply COMPANY POLICY. The thing that separates me from those folks is that I was lucky enough to recognize one thing just as it was happening. And that was . . .

THE RULES HAVE CHANGED.

You'll see that statement highlighted time and again as we go along. It's a vital part of my approach and this book. I'll let you know how the rules have changed and *why* they've changed later on, as well as show you how the new rules work in your favor. I cannot overstate the importance of this.

So, my job as a career coach is to help you to land a great job, a better position, opportunity, and salary in your current job, and reach your potential. As such, I'm a specialist. If you want somebody to talk to about dietary needs, you go to a nutritionist, not a general practitioner. If you need a root canal, you go to an endodontist, not a regular dentist. (As a survivor of four root canals, trust me on this. If you live in Denver, try Dr. Joe Carr.) And if you need career advice, you come to me, or someone like me.

So what can *The Career Coach* do for you? Well, for starters, I can suggest things you haven't thought of, strategies or resources you had no idea were even available. In the last few years, many of my hundreds of clients have told me: "What a great idea. Why didn't I think of that?" in response to suggestions I've made.

See, you don't need to think of these things. That's my job. Your job is to be a great engineer or a great dental hygienist or a great salesperson or software programmer—to be the best you can be at what you do. You don't have time to look down the road. I do. That's why this was written—to help you map your career.

Frankly, you need someone who is emotionally detached from you and your career; someone who hasn't bought into the politics, the emotions, the personalities, the games at your place of work. By probing, listening, and helping you do the research, a career coach can cut through the sludge and get to the real issues. Part of my role is to ask the tough questions and make the tough recommendations.

If you want to prosper, get ahead, and work with a sense of purpose, you've got to focus on your performance. You can't aspire to be mediocre. If that is all you aspire to be, don't waste your time or money on *The Career Coach* or any counseling that costs real money. To get ahead in your career, you need to find out how you can be of more value to your company, at least to *some* company, because that's exactly what *they're* looking for. Companies want impact players: people that add value and bring new ideas to help beat the competition. *The Career Coach* will show you several examples of the actions other people have taken to get to that level.

One of the latest buzz words (or more properly buzz phrases) around corporate America is "core competency." Companies have core competencies. It just means that they're really good at what they do. I mean *really* good. When you think of McDonald's what do you think of? Probably a Big Mac and fries and speed and convenience. That's their core competency, what they do really well. When you think of Microsoft, you probably think of software like Windows or Word. *People* have core competencies as well. Selling software is a core competency. Think of Mark McGwire. His core competency is hitting home runs. Michael Jordan was the most prolific scorer and toughest competitor in basketball. Companies are in such a competitive environment today that they've got to get the most out of everybody on their staff. And the way they do that is by getting people to focus on what it is they are great at. The more you can focus on your core competency, the more money you'll make and the faster you'll get ahead.

I just finished reading a book titled *Lean and Meaningful—A New Culture for Corporate America,* in which the authors suggest that all the downsizing, reengineering, rightsizing, and outsourcing we've experienced throughout the 1990s isn't going to go away any time soon. And I agree. Companies are going to continue to cut back; as a result, they want people who will be highly efficient, very productive, and therefore highly valuable. That's where you, as an employee, want to focus. If you don't, you may well end up in the "mediocre" category. Now there are lots of folks in the "mediocre" category (that's why they call it "mediocre"). Nothing wrong with that. And if that's all you want from your job, you have my complete endorsement (not that I think you need it). But if you want more, if your goal is to improve your career prospects and get ahead, *The Career Coach* will get you pointed in the right direction.

How do I do that? First, I help clients learn the interview process. If you've been out of the marketplace for any length of time, you are probably clueless about current interviewing techniques. I changed jobs four times in the last five years, so I've had plenty of opportunities to be interviewed. And I've talked to countless managers and successful employees. I've learned what to say and what not to say. I can help you in creating a résumé, in establishing a mini business plan, in leaving voice mail messages, and more. For those of you interested (and sooner or later most of you will be) there is more on all this in Chapter 8.

Here, for example, is a quick, short tip on voice mail: Don't leave voice mail messages between eight and five; in other words, don't leave your message during the normal workday. I can remember the nightmare of coming back from lunch and having thirteen voice mail messages. My first instinct was to quickly get through them, giving those that weren't crucial a cursory listen. The best time to leave voice mail messages is in the evening. That way the person they're intended for will get them first thing in the morning when they're at their best, freshest, and least harried. Simple, but effective.

What else can I do? I can help you to develop a strategy to negotiate higher wages, faster promotions, better benefits—the whole enchilada. I'm *good* at those kinds of things. I know what my clients are worth in the marketplace—and often they probably don't. Most of my clients automatically devalue themselves. I promise I won't do that to you. In a recent survey of some seven hundred companies, 53 percent said that they would give employees stock options *if asked* (italics mine). But guess what? Most employees don't know that, and even if they *did* know, they wouldn't know how to go about asking. But I can show you how to do that. I have a good track record in negotiating (a core competency, if you like). In the last ten years of my career, I averaged over 30 percent annual raises. The national average is 4.3 percent. Hey, what can I say? Some things I do better than others. I'm not so hot at golf, but believe me, it's easier to find a good golf pro than it is to find a good career coach.

Some of us don't have a clue about what's going on in corporate America. We may be great at what we do, but when it comes to steering our own careers, most of us are a couple of bricks short of a full load. In truth, there's too much going on to be able to *have* a clue about all the stuff that's going on. It's not merely nostalgia when we think about our parents having a simpler life. They *did* have a simpler life. I'm not sure it was better, but I know it was simpler. My dad went to work in the morning and came home at six every night. My mom stayed home, took care of the house, took us to piano lessons and school events. I don't remember traffic jams or freeway alerts because we didn't have them in the small town in Iowa where I grew up.

But times have changed and (say it with me now) . . .

THE RULES HAVE CHANGED.

We have long commutes, lots of stress, new things to learn like How to Check Something on Your New Palm Pilot While Driving (which adds to everyone else's stress). In some instances, entire new skill sets have to be learned. There's more work, more stuff, more of everything (and, as we're all beginning to learn, more is not necessarily better). We're often trapped by the things we own. In some peculiar way, the tables have been turned so that the things we own now end up owning us.

The old employment model that says work hard, work harder, work hardest and you'll get ahead may no longer apply. A prime example is a client named Scott who was an executive with Polo Retail. He had the great job with a good company, nice house in the suburbs. One morning he got word that corporate headquarters were being moved from Denver to New York. *His* corporate headquarters. To New York! Nothing personal, but New York City wasn't on his top ten list of places where he wanted to raise a family. . . . (He refused to go to New York, though the company did make that option available.) Well, he didn't have a clue about the job market. No clue. Never thought he'd need one. So he hired me. I showed him how the skills he had acquired through the years (people skills, marketing skills, communication skills, planning skills, etc.) would transfer to other companies and other industries. I helped him "repackage" himself and the skills he had developed to better position himself in the eyes of prospective employers. Scott's a very bright guy, but he needed help in this area because he just wasn't familiar with the terrain. He's now a partner in a new business endeavor that requires less travel and gives him more time with the family. His "happy meter" is bouncing upscale. And that's what we want.

There are times when I, too, don't have a clue. Deborah, my wife, and I plan and plant a garden every year. Back when we started, I didn't know anything about gardens or planting. But Deborah did and in effect she became my planting coach, offering tips, insights, practical hints, mapping—all the stuff I can help you with in your career. What she taught me isn't going to get me into medical school (I don't want to go anyway), but it sure as hell made me a better gardener.

A second reason *The Career Coach* is a good investment has to do with research. I'm a huge believer in research. I school all my clients on the role research plays in their careers. Why, you ask? Because it will help you find out what real wages are being offered, what the best companies are paying, what future prospects look like, what the hot markets are, what a certain industry looks like in your part of the country. Though I often work in shorts and T-shirt (at least in the summer), I do lots of research. I'm either at the computer, at the library, on the phone talking to people in the know, doing research, research, and more research. Because of that, I can help guide and plan my clients' careers with insight. I know which companies might be more susceptible to mergers or acquisitions. I can often spot trends in company stock that will have an impact on employees. I'll cover more of this in Chapter 3.

Remember, your nose is to the grindstone, doing your job. My job is to do the research. You need to focus on your job, on getting ahead. I can help with everything else, including "work/life" balance. The number-one objective for most employees is not benefits or training or promotions or even wages—it's life balance. In the bigger picture, the people I work with want to have a job they feel good about going to every day.

A good deal more than half your waking life is spent either commuting to or actually being at work. Yes, lunches count as being at work. So figure a minimum of ten hours a day. If you're not happy at work, the days become ve-e-e-r-r-y l-o-o-n-n-g. Pretty soon you have crow's feet around the eyes from squinting at the clock to see if it's time to go home yet, and permanent frown marks that make you look prematurely old.

If you stay in the "all work and no play zone" long enough, you'll begin to lose sight of the vision and enthusiasm you once had. Pretty soon Jack (or Jill) becomes a very dull person. *The Career Coach* can help you recapture that vision.

I remember the first time I went skiing, in the early eighties. I was with a bunch of other people about my age who were all new to the wonderful world of skiing. We were doing a group lesson. Well, we were all pretty nervous. About a half hour into the lesson, the instructor gave me a tip about how to turn. I don't know if you've ever been on skis, but the idea of just being upright and going in one direction is frightening enough, and actually being able to turn in different directions seems to be something that belongs to another dimension. Or another planet. Well, this guy had this very simple suggestion—that I pretend I have a penny under my big toe; when I want to turn left, I push my right big toe into the penny, lift up my left leg and *voilà! Le turn...*

In no time at all I was shushing down the slopes. I will never know how many falls and sprains and perhaps hospital trips my "coach" saved me from with that one tip. Was it worth the investment? You bet it was. One small tip saved me lots of time, energy, and possibly bodily harm. Now, *The Career Coach* probably can't keep you from bodily harm, but it can help guide you through some of the bumps (or moguls) on your career run.

Dylan had it right—"the times they are a-changin'." He just didn't know how rapidly or how drastically they were changing. And it's not so much just changes in the job market; it's more of a workplace revolution. Next to the hallowed academic dictum, publish or perish, goes a new one—change or vanish (at least from the job landscape). It's easy to quickly become a nonfactor in today's job market.

Take a look at the predicted changes. Fifty percent of the workforce will soon be contract labor. Well paid perhaps, but hired for a definite (usually short) time for a specific task. There are millions of jobs that will be replaced by electronic commerce. It's predicted that within five to ten years, 30 to 40 percent of total sales will be via the Internet. The only constant will be change. (Heraclitus said something about that, but I can never remember the quote.) We need to accept that. We need to get more training on technology; it's going to play a bigger and bigger role in our lives.

Bottom line is that you need a plan. I'll guarantee you that your company has a plan, and if you don't have one, you're likely to be washed overboard when the first storm hits. If you have a good navigator, you'll have a much better chance of not only surviving, but actually prospering. And that's what *The Career Coach* provides.

Chapter One: Exercises

EXERCISE 1 Getting Started

Assign each of the following statements a number from 1 to 5, as best describes your response.

5. Strongly agree   **4. Generally true**   **3. Sometimes, sometimes not**
           2. I don't think so   **1. Huh?**

_____ I love my work.

_____ I understand today's job market, hot industries, and hiring practices, and I am ideally positioned to take advantage of changes and new trends.

_____ I have a range of strategies available to me to get noticed, hired, and promoted.

_____ I know what it takes for me to be a star performer.

_____ I am confident in using the Internet to enhance my career.

_____ I can successfully negotiate a great compensation package with prospective or current employers.

_____ I interview so well, it's scary.

_____ I have an active network of contacts and resources who can make a difference in my career.

_____ I know when to ask for help in my career, and who to call.

_____ I have a clear and specific career plan: I know where I'm headed, and have a strategy for how I'll get there.

_____ **TOTAL POINTS**

Evaluation:

45–50: Congratulations! You have your career act together. You know what you want, and how to get it. Have you considered a new profession as a career coach?

30–44: You have some good skills and knowledge in place, but there's some work to do to move you from successful-by-luck to successful-by-choice. _The Career Coach_ will fill in the critical gaps in your knowledge, bring you up to date, and give you more complete access to the skills that will give you a successful career.

15–29: Career coaching is essential for you. You are probably thinking about the employment market according to the old rules, and (repeat after me) **THE RULES HAVE CHANGED.** _The Career Coach_ will bring you up to date, and show you how to practice some new ways of thinking, do effective research, and get into action about your professional future. Follow the book's advice and you too can become a master of the ever-changing career landscape.

0–14: Your career strategy involves waiting and hoping, occasionally complaining about the ill hand of fate and a boss who doesn't appreciate you. Time to take control of your career, and learn the skills needed to succeed in today's employment marketplace. *The Career Coach* will show you the way.

COACH'S HINT: *For even better results, buy copies of this book for all your friends to whom you complain about your job. Then you can support each other, rather than drag each other down.*

EXERCISE 2

What are your core competencies? List the top three.

These aren't the things you *can* do, they're the things that you can do better than anyone else, abilities that will stand out and be visible to others. If you're not sure what they are, ask people who've worked with you closely.

Entering or Reentering the Job Market

Timing is everything. I'm sure you've heard that before. I was initially going to advise readers that this chapter is designed to help first-time job seekers or those who have been out of the workplace for a few years (raising kids, or someone who was absolutely positive that their garage band was going to be the next Pearl Jam).

But the fact is, there is information here for everyone: first timers, and those who just want to make a change. And since information is power, I'll urge you all to read it.

Most first-time entrants into the workforce are recent high school or college graduates, people just out of the military, or women who have chosen to raise a family before going to work outside the home. Well, let me reassure you, all of you, because I'm here to tell you,

IT'S A GREAT TIME TO LOOK FOR A JOB!

I mean that. You're all entering the job market at a great time. The giant management-worker pendulum has forcefully swung to the worker's side of the scale. In the past, companies seemed to control a worker's future. They determined how much money you made, what hours you worked, what the appropriate attire was, etc. In many ways, they determined your career destiny. There are *still* companies who espouse the old-school attitude that "we own the workers," as there are some managers from the old school who think employees will do what managers ask simply because they are part of management. But such attitudes are fading slowly away.

The bottom line is that unemployment is at a record low and the economy is good and will probably grow for the foreseeable future. Employers are desperate for good employees. It's simply a matter of demographics: There are roughly twenty-five million *fewer* Gen-xers than Baby Boomers. In fact, some experts are predicting that by the year 2005, demand for workers will be up 25 percent and supply will be down 15 percent in the 35- to 49-year-old bracket. That is nothing short of supply and demand paradise.

I began my professional life with the notion which many of you may have shared, that once you started on a career path, you were stuck with it to the bitter end. How you felt about it didn't matter. Say you got your teaching credentials, started teaching, and found out after five years that you hated it; couldn't stand the kids trying to take over the classroom, couldn't tolerate the school board constantly looking for cuts and talking about layoffs. A lot of us felt that if we actually attempted to change careers, maybe from teaching to sales, there was a tendency on the part of the employer to think we had somehow become damaged goods.

Most companies don't think that way anymore. They've had to reevaluate their policies. They've had to do that because the workplace rules have changed. Most of them have realized that the needs of today's workers (more say in voicing one's opinions, flextime, telecommuting, the work/life balance, the ability to take risks and suggest new ways of doing things, more project-based work teams, etc.) are different than they were in the past. Those companies who don't start rethinking their hiring strategies (who they hire, what skills they need, what experience level is needed) will have a difficult time attracting and retaining the best people for the job.

Job Market Research

One of the first things I strongly advocate to new clients is the need to research the job market. (There'll be much more on this in Chapter 3.) Try to find the answers to the questions you most want to learn about a company: Do they share the wealth (are there stock options, bonuses, etc.)? What is the company culture—old-school, top-down, or supportive and open? Do they support the work/life balance ethic? What is their vision for the future? What will keep them ahead of their competitors down the road?

You must spend time researching what's going on in the job market. I don't just mean by going on-line and searching the Internet (although there's great information there). Nor do I mean just perusing books or the latest periodicals (although there is more good information in both). I mean you need to actually go talk to the people in the job market. I call it information interviewing (although I'm not picky about what you call it, as long as you do it). What you'll be doing is talking to employees, and HR (human resources) people, customers and clients, asking about what a particular company is like, what they're looking for, how they're changing, how they perceive the company, and what its problems are.

Before you embark on any new adventure, it just makes sense to do your homework. Even with only a little information, I've got a few more bargaining chips in the employment game. Most of you probably wouldn't think of buying a house or a new car without doing your research. Gone are the days when the real estate agent says, "This house is priced at one hundred thousand dollars," and you are expected to pay it simply because that's the price. Same with cars. Years ago we didn't *know* what a given car cost the dealer. We didn't know what the dealer's markup was. And certainly nobody was going to tell us. Now we do. The information is available if we're willing to do a little research. *Then we negotiate.*

Whoever coined the phrase, "Information is power," was absolutely right. The more information you have, the more power you have. If you know the terrain, the territory, if you, through your research, know where the proverbial high ground is, your chances of success increase dramatically.

So the first step in any job search is *do your research.* This applies to everyone, whether you're a first-time job seeker, someone reentering the market, or a seasoned professional interested in switching jobs. Too often, if you don't do the research, you don't get the job. At least not the good job, the job you really want. Simple, brutal, but all too true. But not as daunting as it may seem at first. After all, I did it—how hard could it be?

How do you begin your research? The library is still a good place to start. Go to the information desk and ask for their help. The Internet is also a great place to do research. If you don't have a computer, use the computers at the library or the nearest cybercafe. Two good sites you could begin exploring are *wetfeet.com* and *vault.com.* Both sites specialize in helping viewers get "inside" info on targeted companies. Plug in the industry or the company you're interested in, and *voilà.*

Career fairs and job fairs can also be useful. In previous years prospective employees went to a career fair and actually interviewed with companies to try and get a job. That's not what I'd recommend. Nonetheless, career fairs are wonderful places to gather information and find out who the movers and shakers are. You can check out the market, discover which the hot companies are—and the ones that might be receptive to new ideas. It's also a great venue to talk to people in the industry. People love to talk about what they do; take advantage of that. A day at a good career fair will provide you with lots of up-to-date information about your field of interest.

I know that when I had a staff, I was always impressed with people (whether they were new to the job market or not) who demonstrated a grasp of what was going on in the business world or the world at large. They didn't have to know everything (and you won't either), but the fact that they knew something about it meant that they were serious about employment. It made me feel better about their chances of becoming successful, motivated employees.

Companies today are much more receptive to new people coming on board who have little or no industry experience. Once upon a time companies wanted only experienced people, and you couldn't *get* the experience because they were only hiring people who already *had* experience. It was quite a catch-22. How am I going to get the experience if nobody will hire me unless I already have it?

But as I said, today you'll find a kinder, gentler reception from the business community. Companies are willing to hire bright, enterprising people who are problem solvers, creative thinkers, who present themselves well and have some understanding of the marketplace (see "Do Your Research"). They will train you or allow you to learn on the job.

Develop a Career Plan

The second thing I tell my clients is that they should start formulating a career strategy. Now, not later. Put an actual plan into place. Document it. Don't inscribe it on stone tablets, because it will probably change. But do put it down on paper so you can refer to it, modify it, and make changes as necessary.

Years ago the job formula was that you got a job with a great company, worked hard, snaked your way slowly up the corporate ladder, and when you were closer to the top than the bottom—success! Employees were confident that the company would take care of them. You might only make one or two job changes in an entire career, or none at all.

Of course, that's not what we find anymore. What we do find are record layoffs in corporate America, mergers, acquisitions, downsizing, and the rest of it that has forever changed the way we look at the workplace. Other strategic career questions now present themselves. Can I move from hot industry to hot industry? How often should I move? What are the signs that will indicate I should make a move? Or at least consider one. Is job jumping a strategy that I can use? Am I positioning myself properly?

Professional sports offers a good analogy. Players go where the market beckons, where there is a need. Such a move may be for a year, or even just for a pennant drive or to shore up a hole in the lineup. If the team doesn't need him next year, another team likely will. Such market pressures influence career decisions, as well; that's why we haven't chiseled the plan in stone.

The bottom line is that today you, not the company, need to be driving your career. So you need to have a plan. Your company does. Guaranteed. And it may or may not include you or your fellow workers over the long haul. If they need to downsize for any reason, you'll instantly be history, hardly a ripple on the surface of the pond. Basically, a plan is nothing more than a map to help you get where you're going. No plan, no map, and you're liable to end up lost and going in circles.

The plan is not going to necessarily detail every career move on a strict time line: which company you'll be working for in a given year, what salary you'll be making, etc. I suggest using broad strokes initially to set up your plan; as you get more familiar with the job market, you can fill in more of the details. Since companies have changed the way they look at workers, you need to change the way you look at your career.

Find the Right Company in the Right Industry

Now is the time to begin to target the industries you may be interested in. Specific companies will come later. It may be that you're not 100 percent sure what your actual skills are, or what you'd really be interested in doing. If so, don't panic; there are steps you can take to give yourself a clearer picture. For example, the Myers-Briggs test is a good self-assessment tool that tests aptitudes and interests. Many local colleges have night classes where you can sign up for this test. Or, you can take a test on the Internet (*Assessment.com* is one such site) that will provide you with some useful information. Another venue you can try on-line is *ask.com.* Type in career self-assessment; you'll get several listings of the different avenues you can try to figure out what will make you happiest. Worst case, the test will confirm the type of job where you will fit in most comfortably. If you wind up in an industry that doesn't fire your rockets, chalk it up to part of the learning process and move on to a company or industry or department that seems to be a better fit.

My son, Brett, is a perfect example of someone who successfully changed fields after a few years. He graduated with a degree in marketing, had several sales jobs where he was highly successful (awards, accolades, etc.), but realized he wasn't all that enamored with sales as a career path. He did his homework, talked to a lot of people, targeted a new industry (high-tech), got some additional education and a new technical certification and he's now happily employed in an entirely new field. It's not the big deal it once was; you can make those kinds of decisions without leaving a scar on your employment record.

The fact is, the job market of today is more forgiving than ever before. I encourage my clients to take a very broad view of their career plan—a global view, if you will. More often than not, you can pick the company you want to work for. (I actually have clients list five to ten companies that they think they'd like to work for.) It comes down to supply and demand again. The company or division or department may not be aligned with your college major. So what? Perhaps you just like the company, or like the product, or like the way the company treats people. Perhaps you've picked a company because you want to make a difference. It's possible. The choices are there.

If you bring something to the dance, lots of people will want to be your partner. But you've got to *bring* something to the dance; some talent, some expertise, some new ideas, something of value (I'll discuss this more later). If you do, I guarantee you that lots of jobs will open before you.

Once you've targeted a particular company, I urge my clients to contact someone who works for the company. I call that person an inside coach. How do you find such a person? Primarily by asking anyone and everyone you know (church groups, athletic clubs, neighbors, cousins, etc.) if they know anyone who works at your dream company. If they do, ask them to introduce you to their contact. Once you've made contact with an inside coach, offer to buy lunch, or dinner, or just get together and talk. Tell the inside coach you're very interested in the company and are thinking of trying to hire on. You'd like to know what it's really like. Make it clear you're not asking for trade secrets, just what it's like to get there at eight A.M. and leave when you're finished for the day. Do they leave at the end of the day thinking "Let me out of this #*&% place!" or do they leave with some sense of satisfaction, a feeling they've put in a good day's work and been properly acknowledged and compensated for their efforts?

Another great question to ask them is what things they would change. That will give you some idea of the company's pluses and minuses, at least from one employee's point of view. As you make out a mini business plan (more about that later in Chapter 8), you'll be able to use such information in an employment interview to show that you've done your homework, that you're coming on board prepared to make a difference. And companies love people who can make a difference. Everyone does.

Whether you're new to the market, reentering the market, or just changing jobs, you get companies interested in you by presenting ways in which you can help make them a better company. Be fluid and flexible. Think in terms of solutions: *How can I make it better?*

Do your homework. Develop a plan. Don't just respond to a want ad, a job posting on the Internet, or an interview at a job fair. Think in terms of the bigger picture and the long term—how you fit in, what new ideas you have that might be of benefit. Even if your ideas aren't dead-on (nobody is expecting you to reinvent the safety pin), companies like idea people, people who think out of the box and have a chance to make the company better by improving a process or a product or coming up with ways to treat the customer better.

New employees should have what I call a "Triple E Rating." They should be enterprising, entrepreneurial, and energetic. Keep in mind that the best employees think like small business owners, rather than employees. The idea is this: What would you do if you actually owned the business? Would you respond differently to some of the challenges? If so, act that way as an employee; that's the kind of thinking that will position you for years to come.

The Loyalty Institute of America (yes, Virginia, there really is a Loyalty Institute of America), based in Ann Arbor, Michigan, found that 53 percent of all workers would be willing to change jobs for a nominal raise. If it takes only a nominal raise to get people to move, what does that say about loyalty? Is loyalty dead? Part of the reason that the percentage is so high is that people are burned out—they've worked long and hard only to discover that companies don't value them. They feel as dispensable as yesterday's newspaper. Most burnout is due not to working long hours or being in a stressful job, but simply being in the *wrong* job. But remember: It's *your* choice! If you're becoming burned out, don't blame it on the company. *Do* something about it!

Another reason employees are so willing to leave is that often they don't feel that they're making a difference, or a contribution of some sort, and the job turns into an exercise in punching a time clock. Now there's nothing wrong with punching a time clock if that's all you want from your job. But for most of us—certainly for me—it leaves something to be desired.

Believe me, I'm not advocating disloyalty. I urge you to be fiercely loyal as long as you're at a company—any company. But loyalty is a two way street. If you find it's not, that too might factor into your decision about whether or not to stay.

In the past, the old gold-plated entree into the inner circles was always the MBA, the business degree from an accredited business school, preferably Harvard or Stanford or Wharton. The degree of the future is going to be the GSD—the "get stuff done" degree. People who can get stuff done are at a premium. Your job is to show your prospective employer you've got the right stuff.

Case Study of Someone Just Entering the Job Market

Here's an example of a first time entrant into the job market— a bright, young, enterprising guy by the name of John Watkins who was a recent graduate of the University of Colorado with a degree in marketing. John didn't know what he wanted to do with his marketing degree, so he came to me for help. He liked technology, so I had him do his research; talk to people in his network, ask them if they have a connection to the high-tech industry, or to specific high-tech companies. I suggested he read all he could about the industry, find out what's going on in the technology field. Remember, technology is not an engineer-only discipline. High-tech companies need salespeople, accountants, marketing people, receptionists, the rest of the normal support staff.

I had John make out a list of the five companies that were highest on his list. One was Quest Communications, a fast-growing telecommunications company based in Denver. Another included Sun Microsystems, which had just opened a plant in the area. He selected three other leading-edge high-tech companies as well, that were well-positioned for the future.

I showed him how to connect with an inside coach. One method, if you can't find a contact through your network, is to call the receptionist at a target company, and ask to speak with someone about the possibility of employment. *You don't* want to speak to someone in Human Resources or the employment office (they'll just give you the company line). If you're interested in accounting, ask to speak to someone in the accounting office; same for sales or marketing. Offer to take whomever you speak with off to lunch, to chat about the company.

John's interest was in sales and marketing, and he hooked up with several salespeople. If you go that route (connecting with salespeople), level with them about why you called (salespeople, for obvious reasons, have great BS detectors). Set up a time two or three weeks out when you can have coffee or a beer together, or maybe take in a ballgame. John ended up getting some great information about what was going on inside the company, what new products were in the pipeline, where they might need help down the road, and who the decision maker was that he needed to get in touch with.

I'm not a great believer in the traditional approach to job hunting, where you fill out a résumé, and submit it through HR channels. They almost always end up at the bottom of a stack that has a half inch of dust on it. In my opinion, résumés are ways to rule prospective employees out, not get them in. If you do your research, locate an inside coach, create a mini business plan (as discussed in Chapter 8) and submit it directly to the decision maker, you'll increase your odds enormously. Now, if they like you, they may still have you go back through channels, but you'll still have already differentiated yourself from other applicants and you will have escaped from the anonymity of the "bottom of the stack."

Because John had been in touch with an inside coach, he found out about a new product that Sun was developing. He did research on the product, checked on the competition, and developed a strategy for marketing (remember that John has a degree in marketing). He wasn't on his own; as his career coach, **I helped him with all that.** Then he found out who the decision maker was, called, and made a mini pitch over the phone. The pitch went something like this. . . . "I hear you have a new product coming to market. I'm a recent graduate with a degree in marketing and I have some ideas about ways to get that new product off to a fast start that you might find interesting." He then went on to discuss a few of his ideas. . . . "Can we talk?"

Remember, there is no need to identify your inside coach. If, during the interview, you are asked how you know so much about the internal workings of the company, the proper answer is that you've done your homework and your research. Which happens to be true.

Based on his phone call, he got an interview (followed quickly by consultation with me about interviewing techniques). The result? He ended up with a position at Sun Microsystems.

Case Study for Someone Reentering the Job Market

Susan Keane was thirty-four at the time she had her first consultation with me. She had been in real estate sales before marrying and starting a family. She and her husband had decided that she would not go back to work until their two kids were both in school.

First thing I had her do was (of course) some initial research, specifically looking into the real estate market, assessing her chances of getting back into that field. She discovered that the market and the job had changed. There was a lot more competition and real estate no longer looked as attractive as she thought it would be.

As a result, she decided she wanted to get into something a little more leading edge. So I walked her through the research process, identifying companies, skills, etc. Susan didn't know anything about technology, and she was wondering how in the world she was going to sell it. But through the research process, identifying companies and talking to inside coaches, she discovered that her lack of an engineering or computer science degree wasn't going to be a big issue.

Eventually she was hired by Hewlett-Packard (one of the top companies she had identified) to call on computer products companies in the Denver area, presenting new products and doing demos for dealers and corporate accounts—and she loves her job. She has better hours than she had in real estate, has more time with their kids, lots more flexibility, all the things she wanted in a job when she did her goal or vision statement (which I'll discuss in detail in the next chapter). She got what she wanted (a great work/life balance) and Hewlett-Packard got what they wanted (a very bright, articulate, motivated salesperson who will do a great job for them).

Summary

Let me just repeat—whether you're a first-time entrant or someone who's been absent from the job market for a while, it's a great time to be a prospective employee. No matter what category of job you're interested in, many of the same tools apply. Just remember: **The Rules Have Changed.** Companies are looking for a different type of employee today. They want passionate, flexible workers, people who embrace change and think like small-business owners. With a little work, and the assistance from this book, you can find a career you can prosper in for years to come.

Chapter Two: Exercises

EXERCISE 1

Answer the following questions, true or false.

TRUE / FALSE   "If I change careers, I will lose all my seniority and most of my salary."

TRUE / FALSE   "Changing careers means I'm disloyal/a malcontent/unemployable."

TRUE / FALSE   "I only know how to do the job I've been doing for the last 439 years. None of my experience is relevant to another field."

TRUE / FALSE   "Work wasn't meant to be fun. That's why it's called work."

TRUE / FALSE   "My employer isn't interested in what I want. He'll just work me as hard as he can."

TRUE / FALSE   "If I'm loyal, the company will take care of me."

TRUE / FALSE   "My major in college determines the industries I can work in."

TRUE / FALSE   "No one will take me seriously if I don't have an MBA."

TRUE / FALSE   "It doesn't matter what I want."

Each of these statements are based on some outdated conventional assumptions about the workplace. If you answered "true" to any of them, re-read this chapter, and write three hundred times, **"THE RULES HAVE CHANGED."**

EXERCISE 2

1. Begin to sketch out a career path for yourself. It doesn't have to be complete, with every "i" dotted and "t" crossed. Just make a start, use bold strokes, and **(this is important!)** be ambitious. Think **big.**

COACH'S TIP: *If you're floundering around unsure of the best career direction, ask yourself this question: "What would I do if I knew I could not fail?"*

2. What industries interest you? Make a list of three or four industries you'd like to research. Describe what interests you about each one (inside coaches and, eventually, interviewers are likely to ask you this question).

3. What kind of company would be the best fit for you? Would a casual, laid-back company bring out the best in you, or would you thrive in an environ-

ment which offers more structure? Describe a work environment which would be fun and bring out your best work.

4. Time for a little research.... Which companies in your target industries offer this kind of environment? Who do you know at that company, who can give you the straight scoop? If you don't know anyone personally, call ten people in your network, and ask if they know anyone who works for your target company. Ask to be introduced to that person.

5. Make a list of ten questions to ask your "inside coach" about their company. Prioritize them in order of importance to you.

6. Who in your network is involved in making hiring decisions? Find three or four people who can answer the questions, "What impresses you in an applicant? What would be an instant turnoff?" Begin to get a sense of the qualities employers are looking for. (Hint: Don't be surprised if you find an echo of the Triple-E Rating: enterprising, entrepreneurial, energetic.)

7. More and more companies are willing to bring smart people on board, even with no experience. If experience didn't matter, what career path would you want to look into?

8. Throw out your current résumé. Yes, that's what I said. (And don't keep a copy in your desk drawer "just in case you need it.") Instead, begin to make a list of your qualifications for the GSD (get stuff done) degree.

   • What have you done for your previous employers? (Emphasize any "home runs" you have hit.)

   • What can you be counted upon to produce?

   • For what business challenge are you a solution?

Five Steps to Getting Started

There's a five-step process that I use when coaching clients. This chapter will illustrate how you can take this same process and apply it to your own career strategy. Keep in mind that the goals, and the needs of each individual determine how much time is spent on each step.

Step 1 . . . Assessment

The basic concept here is that you must know thyself.

Many of us went to college and got a degree, while not quite sure why we got the degree we ended up with. We then began our professional lives as teachers or salespersons or nurses and discovered we didn't like our chosen career. What looked so promising from the halls of academia turned out to be less interesting when we got up close and took a good look at it.

The fact is we all need continually to reassess who we are. The best businesses do that day in and day out. We, too, need to reassess on a weekly or monthly basis not only *who* we are, but our strategies for achieving these goals and *where* we are in relation to our goals. There are certain times when our strategy itself may need to be reevaluated.

Such an assessment may include some type of formal testing (see the self-assessment tools mentioned in the previous chapter). Often, however, just talking about the issues will bring to the surface some concerns or wrinkles long buried and mostly forgotten. Reassessing your strategy doesn't have to be a dramatic (or traumatic) soul-searching experience. But working with someone else may help facilitate the process.

Ask your friends to assess what they believe your strengths and (ouch!) your weaknesses are. Ask for honesty without brutality. What do they think you're good at? Bad at? Do they think you "play well with others"? Or are you better on your own? Are you a self-starter? Easy to get along with? Punctual? A follower more than a leader?

The concept of being a change agent (again, someone who proposes, endorses, and supports change) in today's marketplace is one that is gaining momentum and popularity. Companies themselves have to be change agents; they have to be able to stop on a dime and follow the market. If they don't, they're not going to be in the marketplace for long. Consequently, many companies are looking for people who can respond in kind.

One of the things it's important to discover in the assessment process is whether you are receptive to the fundamental idea of change. You don't want to build a career strategy in the field of, say, technology (where change is the order of the day) if you're not a person who's all that comfortable with change.

It's in that way that your assessment of yourself factors into the process. You've got to be honest with yourself about your needs, wants, and abilities; it is the foundation for the other four steps.

Step 2 . . . Create a Statement About Your Goals

The point here is to sum up what your goal is and put it in a one- or two-sentence statement. It's best to operate on a small scale, at least to start (perhaps you can work on curing world hunger after you get a job).

After doing your assessment, you'll have a better idea of who you are and what's important to you. Maybe money's not the driving force in your life. Perhaps doing something meaningful, working for a company that provides a service that's beneficial to society is more important to you at this stage of your life. Instead of working for a beer company or a bank, perhaps a job with an educational company that provides a needed service is more in line with your needs.

Your goal statement should reflect your aims and beliefs about what you want from a job. If it's money, put that down. It's probably the number-one concern of a majority of people and you're a step ahead if you know that about yourself. As Shakespeare put it, "To thine own self be true." There are plenty of people who want to help cure world hunger. Personally, I think it's a great idea, but I know enough about myself to know that I'm not the guy to do it.

Some people have spent five, ten, fifteen years doing things that perhaps provided a good living, but didn't really fire their rockets. I don't mean they're despondent over it, but they are not living life to the fullest.

I'm a perfect example of that kind of existence. I spent twenty-five years in corporate America, made a good living, got my share of the awards and kudos, but I wasn't really happy about it. After I finally did an honest self-assessment and wrote my goal statement, I left corporate America and embarked on a new career, career coaching. And I love it. I can hardly wait to get up in the morning. I'm really pumped about what I do. I'm in my element, in my zone.

As part of my own initial self-assessment, I asked other people what they thought I was good at, what they thought I wasn't so good at, and what they saw as my weaknesses and my strengths. And I prefaced my questions with the "Please be honest, but don't hurt my feelings" pitch. Turned out they were very open about it, and the one thing that came up time and again was that they felt I was very good at developing other people's skills, and that I ought to do something along those lines.

Step 3 . . . Develop a Strategic Plan

How do you get from where you are to where you want to be? What tactics do you use? What actions are appropriate? Once you know something about yourself and have created a goal statement indicating where you want to go, you need to develop a strategy on how to get there.

Paul is a good example of strategy development. He had a degree in business, got into the job market, took two or three corporate positions while he worked his way up the food chain. He ended up managing an entire division for a well-known company. Then one morning he woke up and, in an unguarded moment, realized that he wasn't happy about what he was doing. For all his experience in management, when he was honest with himself, he realized that he didn't like managing people. I can understand that; I love working with people, coaching people, but not necessarily managing people.

Working with Paul, he and I determined that what he wanted was to be in a position where he was responsible only to himself, and that he wanted to be in a fast moving industry. His goal statement reflected a desire to get a degree or certification in technology that would allow him to enjoy a reasonable income as well as more flexibility and freedom.

If you look at the technology field today, a third of the work force is made up of contract labor, people working on a project basis. He loved the idea of working project to project, deal to deal, taking a month off in between if he wanted to. So the strategy had to address the best way to accomplish that. One of his tactics was to talk to the tech schools in the area, trying to get a feel for what they offered, talking to students in school and those who had graduated in order to get a fuller picture of the strengths and weaknesses of such contract employees. He audited a few classes. He was unsure about whether he wanted to be a programmer or a network systems engineer, so he accompanied graduates in both fields to see how they functioned on the job. He finally decided on being a systems engineer. But it wouldn't have happened that way if we hadn't developed a strategy that allowed him to explore both fields before he plunged in.

A client by the name of Elaine came to me after having spent years in the educational field. It had become increasingly bureaucratic and frustrating for her. During the assessment and goal phase we found that she was particularly interested in being a consultant to corporate America. She could apply her educational skills in helping a corporation (primarily through Human Resources) do a better job of hiring and retaining employees. Of course, she already had experience in developing curricula, being aware of student needs, and so on.

Her desire fit perfectly into the current dilemma in American business of how to be sensitive to the needs of prospective employees in the face of rapidly changing employment practices. We got together and wrote down several ideas about the role she could play in helping them do just that, applying some of her considerable expertise in helping companies out of the familiar rut of doing the same thing over and over while expecting different results. She could help fashion up-to-date methods of hiring, training, *and* retaining the new employees of today.

Part of our strategy was to have Elaine go out and talk to ten consulting firms or individuals in related fields about work conditions, work stability, what they liked and didn't like, the difficulties they faced, and their recommendations. I also had her go out with consultants on assignment to help her narrow the field, giving her a better sense of the kind of clients she'd like to work for. She would also get a chance to see how she liked being a consultant day to day.

That may seem like a lot of work, but embarking on a new career is a big undertaking. You already know that there is no magic wand anyone can wave to ensure it will all come out okay. You'll have to do the research, the homework, and the legwork. If you spend only a dime on preparation, don't expect to get a dollar back. But if you spend an entire dollar—meaning giving your search a 100 percent effort—you might just get two or three dollars back. Life just works like that sometimes. And it's certainly worth some time and effort to land a satisfying position.

Another client of mine, Scott, was Director of Merchandising for Polo in Denver. Through a strange relocation process that the company went through (making the Denver corporate offices suddenly disappear and miraculously reappear again in New York), he ended up being cashiered. As we went through the assessment and goal steps in Scott's job search, Scott decided he wanted to be on his own; he'd had it with corporate America. He came up with a unique concept (a way to merchandise product to increase sales) which he thought he could sell to athletic goods stores across the country. One of the tactics we used was to have Scott go to one or two local sports stores in the area and offer his services gratis. His approach to the stores was this:

I'll come in and remerchandise your golf equipment section for free. I think I can show you how to increase traffic and make more money per square foot. All I ask is that, if you like what I do, you consider hiring me for other departments or other stores in the chain, at my standard fee, of course.

They loved the idea and Scott got to decide if he really wanted to make a career of this. His approach was virtually a working interview, one that both parties benefited from.

I hope you can see how crucial the third step of this process is. It's important to know who you are and where you're headed. But you have to know how to get to where you are going. That's where a lot of us fall short: understanding how we get there, how important it is to have a workable strategy or plan, how our chances of success increase dramatically when we do have a plan. Just as a team may have to change a game plan midway through the game depending on the competition, you may have to change or modify yours. But it's better to go into the game with a plan in mind.

Step 4 . . . Implementation

Step 4 involves taking the strategy outlined in Step 3 and **putting it into action,** which is the only way your plan will produce results.

My client Linda's strategy was to target a particular company she wanted to work for (J. D. Edwards) and try to get as much inside information as possible. She had done her research and heard great things about the people and the work environment. I suggested that, as a way to implement the inside information she was getting, that she connect with an inside coach. She made several calls to the company and was fortunate enough to contact someone in the customer service group who took the time to tell her what it was like to work for J. D. Edwards. The inside coach told Linda where she thought the company was going and made some suggestions about who to contact, and what approach to use as an employee applicant. Later, Linda told me that she couldn't have written a better script herself. Linda got an interview with a company VP and had a job offer a couple of days later.

Another client, Cathy, had a master's degree in journalism, but felt she was unable to get the right kind of assignments from her past employers. The strategy we came up with was to connect with executives in the communication industry and get their feedback on the best way to avoid falling into the same trap with her next employer. What Cathy really wanted to do was help determine journalistic direction, bring in new ideas, be an integral part of deciding what the final articles looked like.

The implementation of that strategy involved making a series of calls to people in her immediate network to find out if they knew any executives in the industry, and if so, if they could help her get an appointment (or appointments, as it turned out). She talked openly about her frustrations in the past, being pigeonholed into positions she didn't like, ending up writing copy and doing other dreary assignments. She wanted a more active role in creating vision and direction for a communications company, be it radio, television, newspaper, or magazine, perhaps even a public relations firm. They (the executives) gave her some great feedback on how to do just that. It opened up a whole new world for her. (Remember: Information is power.)

In the end, she landed a great job with a cool company working with clients, presenting ideas, creating visions for their futures, doing work she considers to be creative and exciting. But all the strategy in the world won't do you a bit of good if you're not willing to go through the hard work of the implementation phase.

Step 5 . . . Support

Some people need ongoing support as they plan and implement their career strategy.

You've heard of GPS, the global positioning system that will tell you where you are anyplace in the world? Think of this step as something similar, a kind of "PPS," or a personal positioning system; its purpose is to help keep you informed about where you are in relation to your goal or vision statement.

Remember, career coaching is not limited to finding a new job. It is also concerned with how to become a better performer where you are, offering advice on how to get along with your boss, how to increase your salary, how to grow and receive more responsibility. The career highway is broad.

First, find someone you trust and respect; I usually don't recommend spouses, as they tend to be too emotionally involved to be objective. What you are asking for is a "change buddy" of sorts. Spend some time each week with this person, talking about where you are in the process, where you want to be, and the distance between them. Talking to someone about the issues involved often leads to the solutions that will help you get you where you want to go.

Case Study #1

A client of mine named Norm is a perfect example of someone who desperately needed career coaching, went through the five-step process, yet wasn't able to go on and apply the principles we had worked on. He simply had a hard time doing it, and seemed unable to let go of old ideas about jobs, companies, and careers that no longer served him well. He had been in investment banking for years, and my assessment of him was that the times had pretty much passed him by. And even though he was bright and hardworking, he just couldn't seem to last with an outfit because he kept trying to use old ideas to solve new problems.

We did the assessment, the goal statement, and agreed on his strategy and implementation, yet when it came time to actually execute the plan, Norm couldn't do it. His head was bobbing up and down in the right direction, but no action seemed to follow. Now *if* he was smart enough to realize he needed a career coach, I kept thinking, and dedicated enough to spend the money to get the help he needed, why couldn't he follow the path we had laid out?

Sadly, Norm serves as an illustration of the fact that career coaching is no panacea. Spending a lot of time (and money) with a career coach is not going to do you any good if you can't implement the strategy you and your career coach set up. If you can't get in motion, nothing will happen. I'm still working with Norm, and I'm determined to help get him over the hump.

Case Study #2

Marilyn is an example of the other side of the coin. She sought career coaching, went through the five-step process, kept moving forward, and is currently enjoying tremendous success. For years she had worked in high-end office furniture sales. She made lots of sales, won awards, earned good money, but she wasn't happy doing it. She had four kids at home, and (even with a helpful husband) she was exhausted all the time. She simply wasn't functioning happily as a Supermom, working ten hours a day, taking care of the house, cooking dinners, and running errands in her spare time. In the end, she wasn't keeping it together.

After going through the five-step process together and helping her think a little bit outside the box, she landed a position as an executive search specialist (a headhunter, if you will) for the office furniture sales industry working out of her home. Her new position gave her the balance she needed. If she had to take one of the kids to band practice at three in the afternoon, she was free to do that. On the other hand, she could sit at the computer late in the evening when the kids were tucked away and catch up. It gave her the work/life balance she was seeking.

She is now making more money, has more flexibility, and spends more time with her family. And she's happy.

And the difference between Norm and Marilyn is the difference between someone who was willing to let go of old ideas and consider new ones, and someone who was stuck doing the same things, unsuccessfully, over and over again, yet expecting different results.

Today's workplace doesn't look like the workplace of ten years ago. And it probably won't look like it does today ten years into the future. Maybe even five years from now. If you're unwilling (or for some, unable) to change, you will likely have a difficult time prospering in the years ahead.

But it doesn't have to be that way. The application of a few principles and the willingness to consider alternate methods will make all the difference in the world. I guarantee it.

Chapter Three: Exercises

EXERCISE 1   Assessment ▷

a) Write down your own assessment of your strengths and weaknesses. Be honest. (Think about how you would talk about yourself to your best friend: You have nothing to hide, and there's no need to try and look good.)

b) Ask three friends what they believe your strengths and weaknesses are, and where they think you'd fit best in the workforce. (**COACH'S HINT:** *Don't discuss and debate what they say, just write down their opinions. This is information gathering, pure and simple.*)

c) Take a big sheet of paper. Write the word "CHANGE" in the middle of the page. Play a game of word associations by writing down everything that change makes you think of, and do it as fast as possible, without editing yourself. Sixty seconds is about right. When you finish, take a look at your associations with change. Are they generally positive? Negative? Do they look like the kind of perspective a change agent would take on change?

EXERCISE 2   Create a Goal Statement

What do you want from your career? Think more about what would really pump you up, not what you think you *should* do.

Your goal is to produce a *concrete, specific* statement that excites you and can be easily recalled. If you're not sure where to start, write down every idea that has any appeal, and ask yourself the following questions about it:

- Would this goal get me out of bed in the morning excited to go to work?

- Does this goal fit my values?

- Would I feel good about what I was doing?

- Would this be fun? What would make it even more fun and more fulfilling?

Examples:

"I earn $100,000 annually providing financial planning to entrepreneurs. I have great professional relationships with all my clients, who consider me part of their core support team."

"I have my own business working from my home, designing marketing and public relations strategies for health care practitioners who are looking to build their practices."

COACH'S HINT: *Don't try and get the goal statement perfect. Just get some ideas down, and see which one lights your fire. If none of them do, call a career coach and get some professional assessment. Many career coaches make their living helping people figure out what they want from their professional life. Don't skip over this one. None of the strategic questions that follow are relevant unless you know what you're trying to achieve.*

EXERCISE 3   Develop a Strategic Plan

How will you get to the goal you just described?

a) Find someone who you consider to be a strong strategic thinker. Take them out to lunch, and ask them the following question. "If you were me, how would you go about achieving this goal?"

b) Imagine that it is a month or a year or ten years later, and you have achieved your career goal. (Congratulations! I knew you could do it.) Tell the story of how you made it. Work backward, step by step, from the successful achievement of your goal back to when you first had the idea.

EXERCISE 4   Implementation

Take the strategy you outlined above, and break it down into action steps. For each step, write down not only *what* you will do, but *when* you will do it.

COACH'S HINT: *People who have a GSD (get stuff done) degree know lists are worthless unless they have a specific timetable. Don't write down the steps on a list. Write them on your schedule. Schedules are the only things that can move our ambitions from "someday" to "now."*

EXERCISE 5   Support

Pick a change buddy. Choose someone who will not be directly affected by your decisions, but who really wants to see you succeed. Don't choose your spouse or your mother. Ask them if they're willing to help, and tell them what specific kind of support would be the most helpful. Do you want a buddy to kick you in the behind when you procrastinate? Or someone to brainstorm or strategize with?

NOTE FOR PROCRASTINATORS: *You probably have all kinds of reasons why not to do these steps. Your reasons (or excuses) are probably very reasonable and logical. And they guarantee that nothing will change. Imagine you were going to talk yourself into these actions rather than talking yourself out of them. How would you do that? What are the compelling reasons to do this now?*

Career Mapping...
So You Don't Get Lost
Along the Way

Just as companies who use a business plan as a road map find the path easier to negotiate, people who use a career map have a much better chance of reaching their destination. If you're in Winnemucca and you want to get to Wichita, a map is a handy thing to have. Without it you might eventually end up in Wichita anyway. Might. Eventually. But it could take a long time. And it's possible you'd never get there at all. The same thing is true of careers. People get lost. Happens all the time.

And, just as there are lots of different kinds of people, there are as many different career aspirations as there are different kinds of people. Consequently, there are lots of different kinds of maps. If you're someone who's motivated by financial rewards, your career map is going to look a lot different from that of someone whose interests have to do with achieving inner satisfaction, or being part of a successful team, or for whom the work/life balance is important.

I recommend that young clients begin thinking of a career map even before they go to college, if possible. I can't tell you how many clients tell me that they spent thousands of dollars and four or five years of their lives getting college degrees and end up wondering what they were going to do with those degrees.

I know in my own case, I initially wanted to be a pharmacist. In my little town of Spencer, Iowa, we had a pharmacist by the name of Amos Bohnenkamp, who was a great guy. Everybody loved him. And I wanted to be like Amos.

My neighbor decided he wanted to be a pharmacist. He invited me down to the University of Iowa to an orientation where I got to visit the School of Pharmacy, and talk to students, to get an idea of what getting a degree in pharmacy was like.

Fortunately, I went. When I got down there it dawned on me that I really didn't want to be a pharmacist at all. Science wasn't a big interest of mine, and yet the degree involved taking a great deal of science and chemistry and physics. It clearly wasn't something for me.

In any event, do get your career map started early on in the process. You want to use the best route to get there, wherever "there" is for you. If you want to be a scientist, go talk to scientists in your field of interest. Try to talk to the movers and shakers, the people who are making things happen as well as the people who do the daily, unglamorous things that make research and scientific endeavors possible. Same for prospective teachers, doctors, lawyers. And you do this precisely so you can discover what you want your destination to be and start making a map to get there.

Making a career map can be beneficial at any stage of the game. If you're just entering the career phase of your life, earlier is better. But even if you're reentering the workplace, or perhaps you've been in your present job for ten years and are thinking about a change, career mapping can be an invaluable tool. Particularly if you are thinking of switching fields, it's never too late to make a map, do the necessary research, conduct a few field trips.

Wherever you are in your career, it is essential that you continue to build a network. Networking seems to have gotten a bad rap in recent years. I think that's partially because some people think networking means meeting someone at a local fern bar one evening and having an empty conversation cleverly disguised as small talk, as you try to figure a way to use this person to your advantage. And I suppose some of that does go on. But what I see successful people today doing is developing a strong network of people both inside and outside their industry that they talk to and exchange favors or information with. Their contacts are usually mutually beneficial. They're give-and-take relationships.

One can label such relations superficial, but such schmoozing serves a purpose. We all need contacts, associates and friends that can help keep us plugged in to the world around us. I tend to view most complaints about networking as sour grapes. And there's nothing easier (or less productive) than being critical and judgmental of others. My hunch is that most people who are burned out got that way not because they were working long hours or having meaningless conversations, but because they're unhappy about what they're doing. Have you noticed that happy employees don't get burned out?

I certainly experienced my share of burnout and unhappiness when I worked in corporate America. And while I worked long hours, that wasn't the principal cause. I now work more hours than ever, but the difference is that I love what I'm doing. Do you love what you're doing? If not, why not? And why are you still doing it if you don't like it?

I often see clients that tell me they don't have time to do the research, the field trips, the work that needs to be done to map out a career. They're stressed out, they tell me. Burned out. Truth is that they're stressed out not because they're working those long hours, but because they're not happy with what they're doing. One of the wonderful things that happens when you enjoy what you're doing is that your stress level goes way down. Another truth is that you don't have time *not* to do the map, the research, and the rest of it. Look in the mirror and tell yourself that you don't mind spending 50 percent of your waking hours doing something you don't like to do. Say it slowly and watch the expression on your face. You probably can't help smiling. Of course you mind.

When I talk about developing a career strategy plan (the infamous map I've been referring to), I'm talking about an actual document. Typically, it's a one- or two-page plan, a summary of your career strategy. Like businesses, which sometimes develop plans that run to several hundred pages, it's a road map, a guide. It doesn't mean you absolutely have to go by that route (that's why we didn't chisel it in stone). If you get to someplace in your travels and the road's under construction, you may have to take a detour. Your company's been sold? Your industry's going in the tank? A decade ago you were working in the oil and gas field? Not to worry. You have a career plan, a strategy, and you know that there are alternate routes available. You know that, of course, because . . . Right, because you've been doing your research.

One of the reasons you're going to fare better than your neighbors is that you'll have learned to look for the signs. Instead of driving right up to the detour and going, "Oh, shucks" (or whatever phrase you use), maybe you've stopped a hundred miles up the road and asked a trucker, "How's the road up ahead?" He just might be able to tell you what's going on. The trucker is the stand-in for your network, your expert-in-residence that you've been talking to—all the people in your industry of interest that you've been checking with.

Too often, I think, we get stuck on a single path and don't think we can deviate from the straight-line approach. That's the Leather Helmet School (Just one more run at the brick wall, Charley, and it'll prob'ly come down). Another thing I hear from clients is a scenario that goes something like . . . "I'm married, I've got two kids, I don't have time to do this, I can't do that . . ." Isn't it someone in *Illusions* who says, "Argue for your limitations and they're yours"? And of course it's true.

I'm not advocating that you quit your job overnight, and sit around waiting for something to develop. But things change quickly in the marketplace. You need to be prepared for that. Make plans.

Have your map ready with alternate routes. Remember Scott Peterson, who had that big job with Polo until the morning he came to work and found out they were moving the corporate offices from Denver to New York? The same thing could happen to you.

There are two questions that I get more often than any others. The first is, How can I make more money? The second is, How can I have more fun on the job? The implication is that the two are mutually exclusive. They're actually not, but it's usually not an accident when they come together. Work and play are two words that we often turn into "either/or" words. Conventional wisdom is that you either work or you play. The concept that work can be fun (play) is an alien concept to most of us. Maybe that's the old Calvinistic streak that runs through the American psyche. And, if you're in a job where you feel you can't move forward, can't change because all those excuses you've been relying on have become so real that they seem like universal truths, yeah, you're probably not going to be too happy about your job. You'll more than likely feel trapped. It's hard to have fun when you feel trapped.

But . . . if a place on your map turns out to be a little less than the oasis you thought it would be, you're free to pack up your tent and move.

The career mapping plan I've developed—and which has worked wonders for the clients I work with—is made up of nine specific steps. I outline these steps below.

The Career Map

An Overview

What should a career map look like? The first step of the career map is what I call an overview; it consists of what you want to accomplish in the near future. (Your vision statement or goal statement has already established your long-term vision.) The career map can look at the next year, the next five years, whatever makes sense to you. You may want to have a five-year plan that you review every year and revise as necessary.

There are times when a career map needs to be changed suddenly. Perhaps your significant other finds a great job in a distant city, or you realize after a short time on the job that you're with the wrong company. There are many good reasons to consider and change your career map.

Your immediate goal might be to maximize the amount of money you make in the next year. Or it might be to maintain your present salary, but spend the year educating yourself about new opportunities in your industry by spending an extra hour a day or so networking, doing research, going to seminars. The summary will help give you a strategy over the short haul.

I worked with a client named Barry, who was a salesman for an office products firm, on career mapping. He decided that for the first year he was going to concentrate just on opening new accounts and building strong relationships. The second year his goal would be to maximize his income. He found out by talking to the experts in the field that his chances of making more money depended on his having a great customer base. So his career map summary laid out his plans to build his account base. Such career mapping or planning may seem simple—and even obvious—but it is effective, and few people do it.

Identifying Your Market

The next step in your career map is to identify who your market is. It's the same step that businesses go through. In Barry's case, once he knew he wanted to open as many new accounts as possible and build solid relationships with those accounts, he knew that he had to do some research on which industries were likely to continue growing and might need his products and services.

The Career Map Marketing Plan

Once you have a summary and have identified your market, you then need to develop a marketing plan. A client of mine named John, a lawyer, was working long hours, not making much money, and quite unhappy. In his overview he wrote that he needed to identify a focus within the legal profession. His market included the top lawyers in Denver. To implement his marketing plan he had to call each of these lawyers and get input about what the best fields were, what recommendations they might have for him, what they saw as the key ingredients to future development as a lawyer.

Identifying Strengths and Weaknesses

Steps 4 and 5 have to do with identifying your strengths and your weaknesses. That's what businesses do as well. The goal is to maximize your strengths and minimize your weaknesses. But first you have to know what they are. Obvious? Perhaps, but few of us do it.

Here's a few examples to get you started.

Step 4: Strengths

1. team player

2. good communicator

3. willing to do what it takes

4. flexible

5. passionate about my work

Step 5: Weaknesses

1. sometimes impatient

2. expect too much of others

3. often want to do it myself

4. don't think before I speak

5. have a tendency to dig my heels in

The Positioning Statement

Step 6 is a positioning statement, which is another thing that successful businesses do on a regular basis. Businesses continually ask themselves, "What business are we in?" The same reasoning applies to one's career. In order to be good at what we do, we have to know what "business" we're in.

The positioning statement spells out "Here's who I am, and here's how I'm going to position myself. Here are what my capabilities are. Here's how I fit into my industry or company."

It won't hurt to think like a specialist. I have a friend who works as a customer engineer for Hewlett-Packard. He doesn't repair computers or widgets; he repairs only mass spectrometers. That's it. It doesn't seem to me that there would be enough mass spectrometers around to keep him busy, but he assures me that there are. And he doesn't repair just any old mass spectrometer either; he only works on one model, which, for argument's sake we'll call the 4000X. If you have a 3000X, he won't come to see you (although he will put you in touch with the 3000X guy). This client is much in demand because he's very good at what he does. He got into the field because some years ago he talked to lots of people who told him that if he really wanted to nail down a good, lucrative position, he should think seriously about learning how to fix 4000Xs. That's what they'd do if they had to do it all over again. This client became very successful, because he did his research, talked to experts in the field, and followed up on their advice to get more training.

The Career Map Action Plan

Step 7 in my career mapping scheme is the action plan. Now that you know what you want to do for the next year or two, you need to identify what tactics you use to carry it out. In Barry's case, once he knew what he wanted to do (increase the number of accounts over the next year), the action plan would spell out how he was going to accomplish that. If Barry had decided that his major emphasis for the year was to make money, his action plan would be entirely different.

Here's an example of items from Barry's action plan:

1. Target 100 companies as potential new clients by Jan. 10.

2. Get names of key decision maker(s) within target by Jan. 20.

3. Send decision maker cover letter and company brochure by Feb. 1.

4. Make follow-up phone call within 10 days of sending brochure.

5. Get face-to-face meeting with minimum 10 decision makers by Feb. 15.

The Career Map Financial Plan

The next step in career mapping is to put together a financial plan to monitor your income, your expenses, and how best to use the funds you have available. If your goal is to build an account base rather than maximize earnings, then you're going to have to think about budgeting money a little differently.

Here's what Barry's financial plan included:

1. Create and track revised personal budget on Quicken.

2. 50% reduction in monthly personal travel and entertainment expenses.

3. A six-month decrease in 401k contribution.

4. An agreement by other family members to adhere to a reduced budget.

The bottom line is that you don't want to be blindsided by a shortage of money when you least expect it or can least afford it.

The Career Map Review

The final step is the review plan. How often should you stop on your journey, take a look at where you are on your map, check weather patterns and road conditions? I recommend that if you're new to career mapping, you do it on a weekly basis. A good time to look at it is Friday afternoon, so you can decide if you need to make any changes for the following week. Once you're more familiar with the process, once a month is usually sufficient. When you're an old hand at career mapping, once a quarter will probably keep you on course.

To sum up, today's job market is changing so rapidly that the people who hope to do well are those who have an idea about where they're going, how they're going to get there, who are willing to put their strategy down on paper and use it as a career map. Just as businesses have periodic reviews about where they are in relation to where they want to be, and make changes accordingly, you need to go through a similar kind of periodic review. If you don't know where you are in the process, or you're not sure where you want to go, it makes the review process that much more difficult. I see too many people making career decisions without a real strategy behind them. It's a little like those who attempt to shoot based on the commands, "Ready! . . . Fire! . . . Aim!" Occasionally you'll get lucky and hit the target, but it won't happen often.

Putting Career Mapping to Work

Laurie was an emergency room nurse when I met her. She was burned out from the enormous stress of the emergency room environment. In addition, she was working all kinds of long hours and she wasn't making a whole lot of money. In making a career map, she decided that her overview, her short-term vision, was to make more money. And chances were she wasn't going to be able to do that in nursing.

In reviewing her strengths and weaknesses, we discovered she had tremendous sales and marketing skills. Following a few of my suggestions, she ended up going to work for a company in a sales position. Her career mapping strategy called for her to learn everything she could about sales in her first year. Rather than go right into outside sales, she decided to take an inside sales position, actually a customer service position, so she could learn all she could about the business. She had a chance to talk to manufacturers, to customers, to people in purchasing, which gave her a great background when she moved into outside sales. Her career map was laid out so that she could progress slowly, rather than jump immediately into outside sales (where the big money was). The slower progression was set up to avoid having her become discouraged and end up quitting. One of her tactics was to network with successful salespeople, talk over coffee or lunch about how they did their jobs, and learn all she could about how to sell successfully as well as about what the pitfalls were, so that in the second year she could hit the ground running. As a result of her well-planned strategy, the year after she got into outside sales she was the top salesperson at the company. That is an example of what career mapping can do for you.

Steve was the president of a major commercial real estate company in the Denver area. He had thirty-five salespeople and did millions in business every year. You're probably thinking, *What does this guy need a career coach for?* He started working with me because he was feeling dissatisfied. He had what so many of us think we want—big job, big money, big image, the entire enchilada. But he wasn't particularly satisfied by his job.

As we went through the career mapping process, we found that he was a great candidate for owning his own business. It was something he'd always been interested in. So his career map began with focusing on starting his own business. The first year (while still working at his old position), he learned all he could about owning his own business: going to seminars, talking to business owners, learning what the upsides and downsides were.

Since he didn't want to compete directly in the market he was about to leave, he decided to specialize. So the second year of his career map was spent deciding what he wanted to specialize in, doing the necessary research and networking. His specialty became working the technology sector of the real estate market. Specifically, he would focus on helping fast-growing, smaller telecom companies find sites to build a switching plant in remote markets. Yes, there were other companies dealing with the technology sector, but nobody was really specializing in this particular segment.

In the third year (this past year) he actually rolled the company out. He's now going like gangbusters, making huge deals with technology companies. Because it's his specialty, it gives him a big advantage over his competitors. He gives much of the credit for his success to career mapping.

Chapter Four: Exercises

CAREER MAPPING

A map is no use to you if you don't know where your destination is. It's time to decide on a destination. These exercises are designed to discover some possible destinations, so you can choose the one that most lights you up.

EXERCISE 1   Where Are You Now?

We know you haven't had a map before, but you've actually been following a default plan which has brought you to where you are now. What have been the guiding principles of your career so far? Is it working for you? What (if anything) is missing in your professional life, the presence of which would make it more fulfilling? Write down a short paragraph which describes the underlying goals of your "default" plan.

EXAMPLE: *I'm working as a stockbroker on Wall Street. I chose this out of college because I wanted to make money and retire at 40. The guiding principles were income and status. It's successful in those respects, but I don't like the people I work with, it doesn't make a difference in the world, and it doesn't permit me work/life balance. If I was making a difference and had work/life balance, my happy meter would go way up.*

EXERCISE 2   The Value-Driven Career

When you're on vacation, you have choices to make. Are you in the mood for lounging on the beach, riding roller coasters at the amusement park, or hiking in the mountains? They're just choices, none intrinsically better than another. How you make them will be based on what you **value** most. The same is true in your career. Abandon the idea of trying to get your career map "right." Instead, put your attention on choosing *the kind of experiences you want to have* in your working life. The career map is simply a concrete plan to give you those kinds of experiences.

a) How would each of these underlying goals change your career plan? Write a short paragraph for each, saying what choices you might make if this was your primary career goal.

1. To maximize your **income**

2. To achieve **status** and authority

3. To have the greatest degree of **freedom** and autonomy

4. To enable the greatest **balance** between work and family

5. To give you the greatest **intellectual challenge**

6. To give you the greatest **personal challenge**

7. To position you to take advantage of **hot industries**

8. To have the most **fun**

9. To **make a difference,** make the world a better place

10. To achieve the greatest level of **security** in your professional life

b) Highlight the THREE goals which have greatest appeal for you, and sketch out a plan that synthesizes the elements of these top three. For example, you might design a plan that would give you income, autonomy, and intellectual challenge (becoming self-employed in a new and fascinating field); or a plan to have fun and make a difference (get hired by a company in a hot industry with a corporate culture that encourages play and creativity, and which has a product which improves people's lives).

c) Imagine you already have this job. What's happening to your happy meter?

COACH'S HINT: *Take your time with this process. Don't settle for a plan which is only a marginal improvement on your current circumstances. Look for something that would be truly fulfilling, enlivening, and exciting to you. If it isn't exciting to you, you're less likely to follow through on your plan. Also, employers love to hire people who are genuinely passionate about their work. If you get stuck at this step, this is a great time to call a career coach who is trained in helping people discover what would light them up.*

EXERCISE 3 Put Legs Under Your Plan

Now you know what you want from your career, the next question is "How will you get there?" The plan, which should be no more than two pages, should include the following elements:

Overview
- What's the aspiration behind your career? Your primary goal? Your mission?

Who is your market?
- Who can provide you with the means to achieve your goal?

What is your marketing plan?
- What will inspire these businesses and individuals to help you/employ you/buy your service?

What are your strengths and weaknesses?
- What are your core competencies? How will you put them to work in your career?
- What weaknesses could sabotage your plan, and what can you do to prevent this?

Position statement:
- What business am I *really* in?
- What is my specialization?
- What results can I be counted on to achieve?

Action plan
- What will I do? What is my tactical approach?
- When will I do it?
- What are the stages in the plan?

Financial Plan
- What expenses will be required to achieve my goal (training, joining organizations, networking meetings, home office equipment, etc.)?
- What are my income goals (90 days, 180 days, 1 year, 5 years)?
- What are my financial priorities? Cash flow (take a higher salary) or long-term planning (take a larger piece of the action in lieu of salary)?
- What is my plan to maintain sufficient cash flow during my career transition?

Review
- How often will I look at my map?
- How will I keep myself on track when I find myself straying?
- Who will be on my "career support team"?
- What will I do to make this career plan fun and energizing?

EXERCISE 4   An Alternative Career Map for Artistic Types

An alternative, less linear career plan is called the Right Brain Career Map:

1. Create a visual representation of your professional future, in the form of a collage of images and words that describe where your career aspirations lie. On one side of your map, assemble a group of images and words for where you are now. On the opposite side, find the pictures, images, and words which describe the *feeling* of your fulfilling career. For example, if your career aspiration centers on a position that is peaceful, prosperous, and creative, find images in magazines and on the Web that capture this energy for you.

2. Your collage should be placed where you can see it daily, where it can inspire you to action in your career.

3. Find images of people doing the kinds of things it would take for you to be successful in your plan. For example, if you need to do lots of research, get a picture of a library and a laptop computer. Or if your plan will require you to get on the phone and make lots of calls, have a friend take a picture of you with a headset on, looking like you're enjoying yourself, and add it into the collage.

4. As your career vision clarifies, you can add additional words and pictures to your collage. It will evolve with you over time.

NATIONAL SALARY SURVEY INFORMATION

TITLE	BASE	BONUS	TOTAL	DENVER 5%
CFO	$82.4	$10.8	$93.2	$97.9
COO	$87.1	$11.5	$98.6	$103.5
Controller	$50.0	$4.0	$54.0	$56.7
Accountant	$34.6	$1.7	$36.3	$38.1
Manager of Operations	$54.7	$6.1	$60.8	$63.8
Manager of Consulting	$69.9	$=	$69.9	$73.4
Manager of Finance	$59.5	$=	$59.5	$62.5
Assistant Controller	$58.6	$=	$58.6	$61.5
Accounting Manager	$68.9	$10.9	$79.8	$83.8

Goal Statement

Career

I should secure a high-paying, upper-level management or executive position with a young and dynamic company.

Coaching

The goal for coaching is to (a) prepare me for a career change, working on my résumé and interviewing skills, (b) to guide me in my search by recommending paths and techniques to explore those paths, (c) help me initialize a professional network.

Strategy

The basis for any strategy should take into account that I have a flexible position, enabling me time for interviews and other endeavors, particularly in the winter.

Strategic Career Change

Step One: Develop skills as a candidate

It is often said of successful politicians that they are better at running for office than serving in it. I have been "serving" for a long time—I just need to develop the instincts and skills necessary to conduct a campaign for a new career.

I should develop two résumés; a "broadcast" résumé, which can be sent to a wide number of places, and a "strategic" résumé—a dynamic document crafted toward a particular situation and presented more in a mini business plan format.

Both résumés should emphasize accomplishments, rather than experiences.

Using the broadcast résumé, I should respond to want ads all over town. The focus here is to (1) learn the market, (2) obtain experience in telephone situations, and (3) obtain job interviews, so as to develop skills in that arena. I should follow up my résumé mailing with phone calls, seeking feedback and information. *The entire purpose is to become more knowledgeable in what hiring companies are looking for— what they will ask, what sort of objections they will raise, etc.*

Step Two: Target practice

I need practice at inserting myself in the nontraditional hiring stream. I should (1) select a small number of companies, fewer than 5, and research them. (2) Of the 5, target 3 for focus. (3) Develop inside coaches at the top 3. (4) Prepare a strategic résumé for the top 3. (5) Arrange an opportunity to present my proposal to the highest logical executive in the company.

Step Three: Find the company

Target my short list of companies in which I have an interest, use the skills I have already developed to obtain an inside coach, present a proposal, and land the position.

Strategic Plan—Rhett Wright

Background and Qualifications

I am a general operations manager/executive in a highly specialized industry. I bring the qualities of organization, focus, and even temper to a dynamic environment. I hold an MBA and possess the self-confidence of a successful businessman. I am an able manager, with a background in competitive sports which lends itself very well to today's concept of the workplace "team."

I have risen to the top of my profession, and it shows in my sense of independence. I am highly flexible, which is good, but that flexibility doesn't extend itself to working in an "inflexible" environment. Give me a position where I have authority and responsibility and independence and I will "get things done." I will work long hours and will be a loyal and steadfast employee.

I am not good at jobs which require a lot of political maneuvering. I probably would not be happy in a sales position, especially if it required me to "BS." I am not opposed to a pay scale tied to concrete results (variable compensation) but I do not enjoy risk for risk's sake, nor socializing beyond a normal day's interaction with people. I can handle number-crunching, but it holds no real joy for me. I am leery of a "9 to 5" job doing the same thing over and over—a groundless worry in today's economy and at the level of authority I would occupy.

I am an excellent communicator and writer. I will come off well in job interviews, especially once some answers can be crafted to anticipated questions (see "Challenges.")

Needs and Desires

- I would like to increase my income from my current level.

- I function best when I feel I am growing and advancing, both professionally and within a company. I would only be interested in a job where advancement was not possible if it were part of a strategic job-jumping framework. However, empty titles hold little appeal to me. I am only interested in personal and financial growth, not a "promotion" to a "Sr. VP" slot.

- I am conscious of the link between my efforts and my success, and want a job where there is concrete evidence of this. I would be very demoralized if I got paid the same whether I worked hard or not.

- I would like to make a change happen sooner rather than later.

Challenges

My sole barrier to entry in any upper-level management position can be summed up in one word: golf. My very first description of my career had the word "golf" in nearly every sentence, and my first attempt at a broadcast résumé fairly *screams* golf.

I must get in the habit of recasting myself in my own mind and learn ways to present my qualifications so that they speak to general business applications.

Reinvent Yourself: Think Like a "Change Agent"

First, a word from our disclaimer department:

So you think you've got a lock on the job market now? You think that all your hard work, your education, and the rest of it is about to pay off like a faulty slot machine? Things are changing in the workplace so quickly, so dramatically, that you may be in for some surprises. This chapter is intended to give you a kind of heads-up regarding what's coming down the pike.

According to a recent *Fortune* article,

"The job is not going to be a part of tomorrow's economic reality. There will always be lots of work, but it will not be contained in the familiar envelope we currently call 'the job.' "

I know we've touched on some of these change issues earlier in the book, but what I want to talk about now is how you can not only survive the changes, but actually prosper.

First of all, the best way to deal with change is to embrace it. Change is the four-hundred-pound gorilla. You're going to be much better off facing it and dealing with it. Change is the one constant we live with. I think it was Heraclitus who said, "Everything is changing, save the law of change." Be smart about it. Don't offer to immediately wrestle with the gorilla. Big mistake. You lose automatically. Be smart. It might be easier to negotiate.

We instinctively have two basic strategies when faced with change or danger or any kind of threat to our well being or security: fight or flight. If you try to run from the gorilla, you lose; gorilla's too fast. If you try to wrestle, you lose too; the gorilla's too strong. What I'm suggesting is a third alternative: Embrace the change gorilla. It's inevitable, so why not, rather than fighting it, take advantage of it and make it work in your favor?

Why is change so prevalent? Because of technology, the global economy, and market pressures so severe that companies have to reinvent themselves on almost a daily basis. What companies need are employees who can do the same. They don't look for people who have one skill, do their job from eight to five, and go home. They want people who will want to improve the company, who want to be part of the company's future.

How are things changing? Well, think commerce for one thing. Starting in mid-1999 e-commerce became something like 8 to 10 percent of our economy. Projections are, that by the year 2005, it will be 50 percent of our economy. When you go from something like a minor part of the economy to 50 percent, that's a huge change. Trillions of dollars' worth. Who would have thought a few years ago that we would be doing on-line stock trading? Who would have thought customers could go on-line and buy and sell products on the sprawling Internet garage sale? Well, of course it's all here now and it's going to change the way we do business. I'm not saying retail stores are going to go away, but they are going to have to change the way they do business in order to compete with folks like *amazon.com* and *ebay*.

Amazon.com started in 1996 just selling books. It changed the way that business operates. Today they're positioned through their e-commerce program and strategic acquisitions to sell anything. They can sell cars on their Web site. They can sell food. Stock. You name it, they can sell it.

iVillage.com is a site strictly devoted to women's issues. If you're breastfeeding for the first time, they'll show you how to do it. Want to plant flowers? Want to negotiate a car deal? There are chat rooms, interactive sites, bulletin boards, everything imaginable at their site.

That's just the harbinger of things to come. The good news is that it's positive stuff for those of us in the marketplace. If you embrace change (instead of trying to do a disappearing act when faced with the gorilla), you're going to prosper: You'll become part of the solution instead of part of the problem, and great things are going to happen to your career.

Making Change Your Ally

Just as companies have to reinvent themselves on a daily basis, we have to do the same. Maybe not on a daily basis, but certainly we need to reassess where we are every few months. Ask yourself, "How can I be of more value to my company or my industry and move my own career forward at the same time?" Companies will quickly notice and reward (with stock options, promotions, raises, perks) those people I refer to as "change agents."

Change agents are the epitome of those who reinvent themselves. My eight-year-old grandson, Brandon, reinvents himself on an almost hourly basis. When we're at the playground or the movies or the mall, I watch how quickly he adapts to the environment. It's almost automatic.

Those of us who are clinging to the old way of doing things are going to be in trouble. There may be a place for us, but we're not going to advance our careers. If just putting in your time is okay with you, there's nothing wrong with that. But I want more out of life. I think you do, too.

The new economy is going to give us a chance to grow and prosper in ways we've hardly imagined. Here are a few examples:

1. We will be able to change careers midstream. We will not have to stay in our chosen field if we decide not to.

2. We will be able to become independent consultants much more easily.

3. We will "propose" work to our current or new employers, thus allowing us to participate in fresh, new work.

4. We will be granted paid sabbaticals in order to recharge.

5. We will be able to negotiate our pay to more accurately reflect our value to the company.

Change is going to be the norm. People who say, "That's just the way it is," or, "We've always done it that way," aren't going to survive in most businesses. We've always known that, but now we're going to see it become a reality.

So how do we become change agents and avoid the job shock that's coming? How do we go about reinventing ourselves?

Think Impact

Think about what will happen tomorrow as a result of the decisions and actions you're taking today. How will what you do impact clients or customers? The best companies will be looking for employees who are always thinking of ways to make the customer happy.

Think Future

We're all going to have to be more proactive. Companies are going to be looking for people who are thinking beyond what's going on today. Whether you're a receptionist trying to find ways to handle more calls efficiently, or a dental hygienist searching for new techniques to benefit patients, the same thing applies. Don't wait for change to come to you; go out and do your research. Be proactive. Be prepared for the future and embrace it.

Think Creatively

All of us need to think creatively. In the past, we had a tendency to think that creativity was the sacred province of some elite cache, at least within the work world. Not so. *We* need to be creative, too. You can't just fall back on the old policies and procedures of the past. The new mantra is going to be: "Think on your feet. Be creative. Find a better way to do the job." Go to your boss with solutions, not just problems. The best companies and the best employees will love you because they love people who remove obstacles. If you're taking down roadblocks, you'll be prized by those above you. Why? Because you're making life easier for them.

"Think Different"

If you're going to be a change agent, if you're going to reinvent yourself, you need to know yourself. You need to find out who you are, what you're good at, what you like or don't like. We're entering the age of entrepreneurism and we're going to have to become experts.

Harry Dent, Jr., author of the national bestseller *The Roaring 2000s*, predicts that we are going to have to become specialized generalists, or generalized specialists, meaning that we're going to have to become experts in our field (or fields) of endeavor. But first you have to know who you are. There are tests you can take to help you to get to know yourself, including a self-assessment test you can take on the Internet for less than thirty dollars. I'll offer a list of such tests later. But I strongly encourage you to take at least one such test. Even those of you who *think* you know your likes and dislikes, as well as the areas you are weak or strong in, may be surprised.

Think About Others

Be sensitive to the needs of others. Try to be aware of the impact you have on the people around you (I guarantee you it's far more than you think), be they fellow workers, management, customers, or clients. Try to understand work and life from their perspective at times. It may help make your own job much easier.

Be Tolerant

Don't be so hard on yourself or others. In any job situation, everyone is all in it together, though it may not always seem so at times. It's okay to expect a lot from others, but it helps to be tolerant, too. Most people do strive to do the best that they can. They may simply not know how to do things better. Keep in mind that any business is more a process than just a single event.

Communicate

Many of us have trouble communicating. Some have a great deal of trouble. There are courses you can take in improving communication skills at local junior colleges or adult education classes. Ask those you work with what kind of a communicator you are. You may be amazed at their feedback. Technology also allows us to become great communicators without having to interact face to face. And there are entire books about how to communicate on-line. You must be able to communicate clearly, succinctly, and quickly to get ahead in today's world.

Here's a few examples of why:

1. Being able to more clearly explain an idea you have will improve its chances for acceptance.

2. Being able to communicate not only with fellow workers but with a CEO or a major client will increase your value within an organization.

3. Being able to use your current employer's preferred methods of communication (voice mail, e-mail) will increase your chances for advancement.

Sharpen Your Business Skills

It's vital that you understand what your company does, how it does it, what your customers do, and how your role in the process impacts them. Too many times in the past we've made decisions as companies and as employees based solely on the short term without thinking about how it affects our customers and our business. Take the time to understand where your company is going, how it's going to get there, and how *you* can help in the process.

Use Technology

It's vital that you improve your information technology skills. Face it: Technology is here to stay. Some of us may be able to avoid it, but we're only setting ourselves back if we do. Look in the Sunday paper and you'll find ad after ad for computer and technical classes; affordable classes. You don't have to become a propeller head to be good at technology. A couple of classes at a local school, a seminar from time to time and you'll be able to keep up. I'm living proof of that. Several years ago, one of my employers sent me a laptop computer to make my life easier, and I let it sit in the box for six months. I was afraid to use it and more than a little embarrassed to be so computer illiterate. Finally, I had an opportunity to sit in on a class and the person sitting next to me gently mentored me into pushing a few of the right keys. Magic! When I found out what the computer could do, I couldn't imagine how I got along without it. I'm still not an expert (and don't intend to be one), but it's a great tool and I use it all the time.

Think Choices

One of the nice things about life is getting to make choices. In business, we get to decide who we work for, how we travel to and from work, how much time and energy we are going to expend toward our careers. We even get to decide how we act and relate to others. The older I get, the better my choices seem to be. If there is an allotment of bad choices, I think I may have used up most of mine when I was younger, because I certainly made more than my share of bad ones.

My clients often come to me with questions about how to improve their careers, how to be happy, how to have fun on the job, and so on. I often say, "Think choices." We have choices today that we've never had before. Those choices will be available for many years to come. Some of those choices are simply due to demographics; there are fewer workers to fill the available jobs, and that opens possibilities for all of us. It's a question of supply and demand.

Case Study #1

Jennifer had been in auto sales for the last seven years, always one of the top two or three in an organization of fifteen to twenty salespeople. She made great money, but she wasn't happy.

When I started working with her, one of the things we focused on was on the concept of reinventing herself, seeing how her skills would transition to other areas. We used the career mapping steps outlined earlier in the chapter and talked about how she could start changing her persona at work. What she was really changing was how she viewed herself, because by viewing herself in a different light, her actions would be different. As each of us see ourselves as capable of doing more, we begin to contribute more at meetings,

bring in new ideas. We'll become that capable person. And the results will be different, too.

After working at reinventing herself for the better part of a
year, she became convinced she could be effective in other fields. She
might have to take home a smaller paycheck initially, but the trade
off was shorter hours and no more nosebleed lunches with high-
powered executives who wanted to know the bottom line every hour
of the day. An easy decision for Jennifer.

She reinvented herself to the extent that she was offered and
accepted a position as the Director of Admissions at a college in her
hometown. She took a slight cut in pay (which she was more than
willing to accept), but there were no more long hours, no more Saturday and Sunday sales blitzes, no more nosebleed lunches with the
ulcer crowd. She likes the fact that there is balance in her life today.
And she continues to practice being a change agent, for herself and
for others.

Case Study #2

Jim was a client who had been in purchasing for a major manufacturer for a number of years. He was working his way up, getting
raises, good reviews. He was even made Director of Purchasing. But
when he came to me he had decided he wanted to go to work for a
different company because he wasn't particularly happy where he
was. He needed some direction about the best way to go about
changing companies.

As we started talking during the assessment phase, it turned
out that though he was good at purchasing, he wasn't crazy about it.
So we talked about reinventing himself, and discovered that he
really did like the company, he just didn't want to be in purchasing
anymore. Since he had always liked marketing, he went back to the
company with a proposal that would allow him to transition into
marketing and take on a couple of different roles. Drawing on his
experiences in purchasing, he had some ideas of how to market
some of their new products. The company loved his ideas and was
willing to give him a shot at a marketing position. That was about a
year ago, and he has since had two promotions, and is happy and do-

ing well. One of the things he tells me is that by becoming a change agent, and being willing to think of himself in a different light, he's moved around within the marketing department. As a result he doesn't just do the same job every day; he's been allowed to work on different projects. He's brought new ideas about advertising and promotions, about new projects, and brought new energy to the department. Every day is indeed a new day for Jim, and he loves it.

Chapter Five: Exercises

EXERCISE 1 Do You Think Like a Change Agent? ▶

5. **Strongly Agree. This describes how I think about my career.**   4. **Mildly Agree. I think this way most of the time.**   3. **Erratic: I sometimes do this, sometimes not.**   2. **Rarely. It doesn't usually occur to me to think this way.**   1. **Huh? I never think about this.**

_____ I make choices today with awareness of their long-term impact on my career and my company.

_____ I am able to reinvent myself to meet changing needs in the workplace.

_____ I consider no business process to be carved in stone. I proactively look for opportunities for improvement wherever I go.

_____ I find obstacles to remove, and implement strategies to remove them.

_____ I have abandoned *hoping* for a better future. I have a *plan,* and I take *action.*

_____ I know what I'm good at, and I know what I love to do. These are the foundations of how I operate at work.

_____ I cultivate my professional relationships by practicing tolerance and open communication. I don't avoid difficult conversations or gloss over differences of opinion.

_____ I am aware of how others perceive me, and the impact I have on my colleagues.

_____ I know how my work impacts the success of the business.

_____ I upgrade my tech skills through classes and trainings at least as often as I upgrade my computer software.

_____ TOTAL POINTS

40–50: You are a change agent. You will make a difference wherever you go. Chances are, your employer will do a lot to keep you on his team if you keep operating this way.

30–39: You have what it takes to become an effective change agent. Your next task is to identify the places where your thinking has not yet aligned with this, and upgrade it. See the exercises below.

15–29: You are suffering from an "old rules" hangover, or you're working in an "old rules" organization. You have expectations that no longer apply to the new economy and new workplace. If you want proof that these characteristics are valued, ask your boss how you can be more effective and make more of a difference. See what he says.

0–14: This is new to you, isn't it? If you want to become a change agent, get a career coach who can walk alongside you as you discover a new and more effective way of operating at work. If not, put down the book, and return to your couch (or cubicle). Being a change agent requires work, and you have to want it.

EXERCISE 2 Exercises to Develop the Skills of a Change Agent ▷

A) Assess how your actions affect your company's business, if necessary by asking your boss for his opinion. Where is there room for improvement?

B) What are you hoping might happen in your career? What action could you take now to increase the chances, or, better still, stack the deck in your favor?

C) What would be a better way to do one aspect of your current job? Find an obstacle to remove.

D)

- What are you really good at? What do you love to do?

- How can you work these into the daily fabric of the job you have?

- If you can't see a way in your current position, what work environment would value and reward these kinds of skills?

E) What impact do you have on your colleagues? Write down what you think about yourself, and then go interview at least three colleagues. Listen for consistent themes in what they say.

COACH'S HINT: *Be willing to abandon any ideas of how you are perceived if they are not shared by your colleagues. Build around the strengths that other people can see.*

F)

- What will trigger you to judge others negatively? (Laziness? Gossip? Illogic?)

- What impact do you think your judgments have on your coworkers?

- What impact do your judgments have on *your* effectiveness?

- What will consistently trigger self-criticism in you? (Looking foolish? Missing a deadline?) What will it take for you to learn from these situations, forgive yourself, and move on?

G)

- Ask a colleague to assess your communication skills. Do they understand you when you talk?

- Find a communication buddy. When you have an important proposal to make or an interview, practice with a buddy. Focus less on content, and more on the clarity and economy in your speaking.

- Find at least three classes on communication skills. Take a minimum of one per year.

H)

- Where is your company going? What is its strategic plan? How do you contribute to it? If you don't know the answers to any of these, *ask*.

- From your research, identify three ways to ensure that your work makes the maximum impact.

I)

- What tech skills would make you more effective in the workplace? What skills would make you more marketable?

- Find out where you can take these trainings, what different schools offer, calculate your personal tech training budget, and sign up for *at least one class per year.*

COACH'S HINT: *Don't ask the tech schools what skills make you more marketable. Ask employers and recruiters. Some of the more unscrupulous tech schools will push you to take certain courses within their curriculum, which may not necessarily provide you with the skills employers want.*

J) Identify and take *three* actions you could take in the next thirty days which will move you closer to achieving this goal. Take those actions!

How to Improve Your Job Performance (and Become a Star!)

One of the questions I get most often from clients, prospects, or people who listen in to my career coach radio show is: "How do I create the happy, successful career you talk about?" The truth is, there are lots of ways: Finding balance in your work/life situation, or doing something you love (or *like* at the very least) are only two examples. But *the* single most important way, in my opinion, to create that successful, rewarding career I'm always talking about is to be a star performer at work.

And when I say that, people tend to look at me as if I can't be serious. "Sure, easy for you to say," they often say, "but I'm not a star." They recognize the truth in my statement, but simply don't think it applies to them. We apply the term "star" to those who are highly visible and successful people at work, in sports, or entertainment. But I'm not talking about being a Michael Jordan, a Bill Gates, or a Steven Spielberg at your job. What I'm referring to is about being a star performer at the level you're playing on. If you're playing Double A baseball, you don't have to do the things a major leaguer does in order to be considered a star. It's the same in the business world; being a star performer may mean being an outstanding performer in your little niche of your company. You don't have to get write-ups in *The Wall Street Journal* to be considered a star.

In my own career, becoming a star performer, whether it was in my department or division or company, had a ripple effect. It wasn't just the big raise or the big promotion that went with it (although that was certainly part of it). More to the point, it impacted the way people looked at me, how they talked about me, how I was viewed by management *and* clients. It opened doors. The walls that had kept me from access to other people simply vanished. I wasn't any different, I was still Gordon Miller, a guy from Iowa. But I was viewed by others as someone to watch, someone on the move, someone you could give an assignment to and know that it would be done and done well. And I made sure that it would.

So there's no deep, dark secret to being a star performer. Most everyone can achieve it if they understand the components. So why don't they? The truth is that most don't know how. Others don't care about becoming a star. To many people a job is just a job. It has not occurred to them that the workplace can be a place where they not only make money but also have fun and enjoy themselves. We have all too often latched on to the notion that work is drudgery. It may be for some, but it doesn't have to be. And the very fact that you bought this book and are studying its contents is evidence that you care, and do want to know how to be a star.

Can the majority of people in the workforce become star performers? The answer is yes. I've seen people who have been described as not being smart enough to succeed, not working hard enough to succeed, not being motivated enough to succeed, yet that is what they have done.

Almost everyone can become a star performer.

Everyone? Probably not.

The majority of people who want to, actually can become star performers. Even if you've never been a star performer in the past, such performance is not out of reach.

When I attended my twentieth high school reunion, I was surprised to find that the star performers in school (with a few exceptions) didn't turn out to be the star performers in the game of life. The president of our senior class was a straight-A student, had won honors galore, was a cheerleader, and so on. Later in life, however, she had had some very difficult times, and even attempted suicide at one time. The past is no guarantee of success, or *lack* of success.

So how do you become a star performer? Does it mean you have to eat, sleep, and live your job twenty-four hours a day? Sure, it takes concentrated effort at times, but it doesn't mean you have to work twenty hours a day.

The Carnegie Mellon Institute out of Pittsburgh, Pennsylvania, recently conducted a yearlong survey of seven hundred companies, checking with top management about the habits and characteristics of people they considered their star performers. Here are just a couple of what at first seem like startling results.

Star Performers Are Usually Not Geniuses

The Carnegie Mellon report showed that star performers had a *lower* IQ than the average worker. Incredible? Perhaps. But I suspect the more you think about it, the less incredible it seems. We've all known people who've struggled in school, or on the job, and later just blossomed into star performers. I just have to look back on the years I coached baseball. The kids who made it to the next level, whether in high school, college, or the minor leagues, were often *not* the people with the most talent. I've often wondered why. The only thing I can come up with is that sometimes the struggle itself ("I don't have all that natural talent, so I have to work for what I get"), does something to toughen people up for the task ahead. Years ago they probably called that "moxie." I don't know if we've got a word for it today.

I love to quote that statistic because it gives guys like me a boost. It means I don't have to have an MBA or have an IQ that's in the high triple digits. I don't know about you, but my name was not permanently etched onto the dean's list when I was in college. I was a very average student. Here is the second statistic from the Carnegie Mellon survey:

You Don't Have to Work 18 Hours a Day to Be a Star Performer

On average, the star performer worked *fewer* hours than the average performer. That's encouraging because, in other words, you don't have to dedicate every waking hour to the company in order to become a star performer.

Why is it so valuable to be a star performer? For one thing, people who are star performers are self-confident—they have about them an air of confidence. They understand that they are going to make mistakes, that they aren't going to win every deal, but they have confidence that they know they don't have to win every deal to be successful.

Moreover success breeds success. It seems to be one of those strange rules of the universe that good things happen to people who are doing good things. The converse also seems to be true; if you're on your way down the ladder, half the rungs are going to be missing. There's an old saying that "The rich get richer and the poor get poorer." There may be more truth here than poetry.

A third reason why it's so valuable to be a star performer is that winners like to do business with winners. You don't want to get your car worked on by a mediocre mechanic, do you? Neither do I. When you are successful, other people who are successful naturally start gravitating toward you.

Bottom line? Stars make more money, tend to be more satisfied, and have more fun.

So just how *do* you become a stellar performer?

1. Think in terms of small steps. Nothing is truer of the process. You eat the elephant one bite at a time; if you're smart, one small bite at a time. Whether you're a financial planner, a busboy in a restaurant with aspirations to be a waiter, a teacher, a salesperson, or a mid-line manager, don't think it's going to happen overnight. That's simply a great setup for failure, because you're not going to achieve what you want to as quickly as you want to and you're going to end up frustrated and discouraged. Take small steps; you'll be much better off in the long run.

2. You must continue to do research on a regular basis. Twenty to thirty minutes a day is usually sufficient. Take the time to read a relevant periodical, scan the Internet for information pertaining to your job, talk to others in your field. There's some great information out there about what's going on in the marketplace. Keep up with the latest books on your industry. The main thing is to do daily research on your industry; you'll be surprised how it's going to help you in the future. And the reason you'll be surprised is that most people don't do it. You may well turn out to be the only kid on your career block who knows what's going on in your area of expertise.

3. The third step is that you ask management in your company what you can do to make yourself more valuable. Go to them proactively and say, "I'd like to be more valuable to the company. How do I go about doing it?" That accomplishes a couple of things. It lets management know that you're serious about your career, and it earns you some gratitude that will come in handy at some future time.

4. Ask for assignments nobody else wants. There are always those unglamorous tasks that no one wants to do. Maybe

they take too much time, they're hard to do, they're thank-less, whatever the reason. Ask if they need some help with quarterly reports, or the inventory, things that people find time-consuming and boring. I'll guarantee you you'll get to help. And it is a surefire way to make yourself into a star performer.

5. Present management with a plan to improve problem ar-eas at work. We all know what the problems are. After all, we all like to bitch and complain about them. But how many of us are willing to do anything about them? Well, the star performers come up with ideas or plans to improve those problem areas. I'm not talking about a fifty-page document to be published in a journal. A one- or two-page memo saying, "Hey, I think we have a problem here and this is what I think we can do about it." Maybe it's a plan to reduce accounts receivable, or just some way to ensure that incoming phone calls don't get lost between the cracks.

6. Offer to assist fellow employees on their projects after hours. Obviously you have to use work time for your own work and projects. Just be careful you don't get too dis-tracted; you can spread yourself too thin. But you can offer your assistance selectively. Maybe someone's been out sick a couple of days, just bogged down, maybe someone in cus-tomer service has been asked for a bunch of reports and doesn't have time to do anything else. Just go to that person and say, "I know you're buried in stuff this week and I've got a couple of hours after work on Thursday. Okay if I give you a hand?" That person will never forget you. Never. Guaranteed. And he or she will tell at least a half dozen people about it.

7. You know the daily "to do" list that so many of us make? Then proudly smile as we take things off the list.... *That's done. That's done. Boy, I feel good. Only nine more to go...*

Well, star performers put things *on* the list. They don't focus primarily on taking things off (though that obviously gets done); they focus on what other things they can do.

8. Give others the credit when things go well. Of course it's possible to overdo something like this and if it becomes insincere, people know it and become resentful. But at the appropriate time, when the situation calls for it, give other people the credit, even though you may have been the main architect of the success. Why? Because you'll find lots of people who want to get on your bus, who'll want to be part of a good thing, part of an experience where they feel valued. Oh, you'll find the occasional employee who is resentful or envious. It is, perhaps, an unavoidable part of your journey.

But if you stay focused on the process, on the little things that engender success, you *will* become a star performer. That is the way to start building confidence, so that you believe it's possible to improve not only your work performance, but your work/life balance as well. When people ask about the work/life balance I simply tell them that if things are going really well in one part of your life, chances are good that that outlook will spread into other areas. We certainly know the reverse is true; if you're having a terrible time with your significant other, or with some outfit trying to repo your car, that sense of gloom is likely to spread to your work as well. And of course if you're having an awful time at work (remember how much of our lives we spend there?), chances are good that your home life will be affected as well.

As you begin to put the above steps into action, you'll begin to understand that you really don't have to be a rocket scientist or forfeit every waking hour to your job to excel at work. But how do you maintain that self-confidence over a period of time?

There are a couple of other key things I see star performers do that we can all learn from. First, they have a better sense of understanding which relationships are important to their careers and which ones aren't. Who you associate with has a tendency to reflect and determine what your performance is. Oh, you can be a star performer on a bad team, but your chances are much better on a good team. That may seem a little at odds with what you've been taught. Conventional wisdom has it that it is easier to stand out as a top performer in a small (read: second-rate) pond. Not in business. It's easier to do well when your company, and those around you, are good performers.

Some relationships can help you in your career and others can't. People that are energy draining (or energy dependent) fall into the latter category. Now there's nothing wrong with giving people a power boost from time to time (actually that's a *good* thing to do), but people of the "energy drain" persuasion can never get enough. You'll get run down and they'll still be needy. You will not have helped them; they will only be more convinced than ever that they need you. While that may be flattering to your ego, it's not going to do a thing for your status as a performer at work.

You want to focus on relationships where there's a positive energy exchange. You do great things for people; they do great things for you. That's the equation to focus on.

Top performers also tend to streamline the number of people they work with. That doesn't mean you have to stop talking to people in the hall or ignore those around you. But it goes back to the old 80/20 Rule. Eighty percent of our success comes from 20 percent of our efforts. You need to nurture those relationships that represent the 20 percent. You cannot be all things to all people (somebody famous said that, but I can't remember who).

Being of service or of use is a tremendous positive as long as you don't overcommit yourself; it builds momentum and self-confidence, two important ingredients in a top performer.

But if you're going to be a partner (either with your company or fellow worker), be a good partner or don't be one at all. My own experience tells me that sometimes, when I'm working with a client, or working on a business deal, the fit just isn't there. For whatever reason (and some of them may be hidden) we weren't able to form a partnership that did either one of us any good. I've had to go to those people and say, "It's just not working. I can't hold up my end of the bargain and do what I said I could do. It's best we put it on the back burner for now. Maybe even off the stove." That's being a good partner. It's being open and honest about what you can do and what you can't do. People respect that. What people don't respect is when fellow employees say they're going to do something, don't follow through, and then offer all kinds of excuses about why they couldn't get it done. You'll be far better off by being open and honest and up-front.

A final thought about relationships and the part they play in becoming a star performer. Some of my clients ask me about jealousy or envy and how to deal with it. Not pretty emotions but unfortunately fairly common in the workplace where some people get ahead faster or at a younger age than others. I suggest you need to deal with it head-on. Take the person to lunch, to coffee, address it. Something like, "I understand from the grapevine that you're a little miffed over my promotion. I just want you to know that I understand the feeling. When Frank got his promotion last month I was more than jealous myself. I went to him and more or less told him so. And I ended up asking how I could learn from his success. It turned out to be a great conversation." Essentially what you want to do is defuse the situation. Take action. If you don't, the jealousy will turn into anger, which will turn into resentment, and then everybody loses. Deal with the situation and move on.

Once you're building positive relationships and beginning to see the benefits, what are the things you can do to advance to the next level? Have a clear road map, stay focused, and try as much as possible to be detached from the results.

Don't Focus on Results

You must keep focused on the process, on doing the small things right every day. The results will come. Believe me.

If you're a secretary and your goal is to handle each call in under thirty seconds, you might end up alienating more than a few customers in your quest to get them off the phone just to meet the goal. And remember those ads about getting your pizza in less than thirty minutes? It seems to me it's a sure-fire way to increase accidents and speeding tickets, all to ensure an intermediate goal. What's the real goal? Customer satisfaction. Stay focused on that.

Top performers ask for help when they need it. They ask for feedback in an effort to improve their performance. Remember that what you do determines where you end up on the corporate ladder.

Case Study #1

Barry was what you could generously term a mediocre salesperson. I worked with him when I was still a senior manager in the corporate world. He was a likable guy, worked long hours, but never seemed to have great success. We first worked on getting him focused. Barry was the classic example of someone who spread himself *too* thin. He helped everybody. We worked for an office products distribution outfit and Barry would work the phones, help in the warehouse, unload trucks, anything and everything. Now there may be times when it's necessary to do that, but if you do it all the time you're not helping anyone. What happens is that your own sales go down, there's less stuff in the warehouse and less stuff on the truck.

We worked on controlling how much time he spent on his own business, while still finding time to help out others here and there. As you might imagine, Barry has great people skills, and everybody loves him. But now he's proportioning his time properly. As a result he's more focused and he's a lot more effective. And he's now one of the top salespeople with the same company. Just a small adjustment, but a big payoff.

Case Study #2

The second case study is a dental hygienist who wanted to move forward, but felt stuck in her job. Some jobs tend to have built-in limitations and dental hygienist happens to be one of those. If you don't want to go back to school and become a dentist, there's only so much room in which to maneuver. She wanted to make more money, have more interesting cases.

I suggested she go take some night courses, study new techniques, new concepts in hygiene, just see what was available. She started doing her research (you remember—research, research, and more research) and discovered that there *were* new services available that hygienists could provide. So she went to her boss and simply said, "I can be more valuable to you if you'll send me to this school" (root planing, I think, but don't hold me to that). "We can provide additional value *and* increase profits by making this service available to our customers."

The dentist thought it was a good idea (who wouldn't?) and sent her to school. They increased their customer base, she became the lead hygienist, and ended up getting a percentage of the root planing business. Positive thing for everybody. The classic win/win scenario we all look for.

The biggest obstacle to overcome is the belief that we're not capable of being more than we are or doing more than we do. The old bromide about creating your own life experience holds true for your job experience.

Stop Underestimating Yourself

S tart doing the small things we talked about. That will give you the confidence to move forward toward creating a positive job experience. You can do it. I've seen thousands of people do it, some certainly no more talented than you. It works. Go for it!

Chapter Six: Exercises

BECOMING A STAR PERFORMER

"What me? A star performer? Who am I to be a star?"

The very idea of becoming a star performer has you squirming, doesn't it? So before we learn about what it takes to become a star performer, let's look at your resistance to becoming a star performer. (No need to get deeply psychological here: We just want to know what might stop you.)

Introducing the Inner Critic

We all have a running commentary going on in our heads, providing us with negative opinions about our work, our life, our appearance, our overall worth as a human being. It's the voice that says, "You didn't do that quite right. Someone else could have done it better. And your hair is a mess, by the way." That commentary is being given by your inner critic.

The more an action has the potential to create change, the louder your critic will become. Your critic won't offer an opinion about which brand of mayonnaise to buy at the grocery store, but when you consider offering an innovative proposal to your boss or looking into a new career path, be ready for a critic attack. "Who are you to share your ideas? No one wants to hear them, and you'd better not share them, because your boss is bound to say no, and then you'll look foolish." The critic wants you to believe that the only possible outcomes are embarrassment, loss of respect, and, knowing your luck, getting summarily fired.

The critic speaks with such authority that it really does sound like it is speaking in (capital T) Truths handed down from on high on stone tablets. In actuality, the critic simply offers one scenario, usually the worst case. Such a proposal might equally well lead to a bonus or a promotion, but your critic will never suggest that. The critic will declare, "It's bound to fail because it's *you* doing it, and you're bound to screw it up! Just look at what happened when you asked that pretty girl to dance when you were 17. She said no, and you felt really bad. Want to go through that again?"

When we listen to the critic, what we get is the status quo, because *any* change feels like it might threaten the security and success we have. There's not necessarily anything wrong with the status quo if it's working for you, but I have a hunch that if you're reading this book, you want more from your career than you have at the moment. More means change, and effective change means taming that critic.

EXERCISE 1

Your job is to identify the voice of your critic, so that when he shows up, you know what to do. Here's how to identify that your critic is present:

Is your career directed by your critic?

1. When you talk about your career, the words, "should, must, have to, and can't" show up all over the place.

2. You don't like where you are, but you feel afraid to change it.

3. You think all the time about what to do next, but you do not take any action.

4. When you start to think of a better future, you find yourself thinking, "It's not too bad where I am. I can stick it out a few more years. I could do worse." (The critic will talk you into settling for an unsatisfying life, and tolerating the intolerable.)

5. You see problems and potential pitfalls in every plan you make. You're so aware of what might go wrong, that you find it hard to even see what might go right.

6. You can talk yourself out of anything that might change the status quo.

7. You're very concerned about what other people may think. Would they think you were foolish to change careers? Misguided? Gullible?

8. You argue for the old rules: it has always been this way, it will always be this way. You're basically powerless to change anything, a passive victim of market forces and corporate culture.

9. Being a star performer is for people with more talent than you. The career coach must be talking about the kind of people who got straight As in college and have been on the fast track ever since. Not me.

Your critic will **never** agree that you could be a star performer. Never. Don't try and convince it, since it will tell you all the reasons why you can't. In fact, your critic will resist most of the new ideas in this book (particularly "The rules have changed").

EXERCISE 2   How to Silence Your Critic

Your critic will always be there, offering you his commentary. Silencing the critic is impossible (there's probably something hardwired into being human about fear of change). However, once you recognize that, despite the authority of the critic's voice, what he says is simply a point of view and not the (capital T) Truth, it's possible to put his opinions aside, and choose again.

Do *not* try and please your critic. It's impossible. Nothing is ever good enough for a critic. (A client of mine said that her gremlin was just like her mother: If she got an A in a class, her mother would ask, "Why didn't you get an A+?")

When you notice your critic speaking, say, "thanks for sharing" and look for another way of looking. If the critic represents pessimism and fear, what would an optimist say about this situation? If you can find another perspective, you automatically separate from your critic, and he loses power over you. Try using the perspective of a change agent or star performer: "What would a change agent do in this situation? What would a star performer do?"

You need to know, by the way, that the critic is universal. In other words, *everyone* is afraid of not being good enough, smart enough, slim enough or hardworking enough (even star performers). Star performers are the people who are able to take action in the face of their fear, rather than being paralyzed by it.

COACH'S HINT: *Experienced critic tamers know that when the critic is loudest, you're on to something: The idea you just had or the option you're considering has the potential to create real change in the status quo.*

EXERCISE 3

For one week, *pretend* to be a star performer. (Even if you don't feel like one.)

Here's the star performer formula. Practice as many of these steps as you can this week (if you don't apply all of them, it's okay, no matter what your critic may say . . .).

- Think small steps.
- Take your time.
- Do your research.
- Ask management what you can do to make yourself more valuable.
- Ask for assignments no one else wants.
- Create plans to solve problem areas at work.
- Assist colleagues who are overwhelmed.
- Add things to your "to do" list. Expand the range and scope of your impact.
- Give others the credit.
- Focus on the important relationships.

- Focus on process, not results.
- Stop underestimating yourself.

During this week, keep track of the following:

1. Count the number of times your critic showed up. If you are like most people, you'll lose count before the end of the first day practicing being a star performer.

2. What did your critic have to say? Does he use the same stick to beat you with all the time, or does he have a range of weapons at his disposal?

3. Which aspect of being a star performer got the critic most agitated? THAT IS THE ONE WHICH HAS THE POTENTIAL TO MAKE THE GREATEST DIFFERENCE IN YOUR CAREER!

4. When you get a positive outcome from one of your star performer actions, what does your critic say about it? How does he try and discount it?

5. When you succeeded in meeting a goal your critic said was impossible, did he shift his attack to another area?

By the end of the week, you will see that your critic has a distinct personality and a couple of consistent ways of making you really afraid. If there's one thing to learn from this whole exercise:

It is your critic, not you, who is resistant to your becoming a star performer.

You want a great, fulfilling career where you get to fulfill your potential. *Your critic wants the status quo.*

You want to get on the basketball court and make a difference, be a player. *Your critic wants to sit in the stands, making cynical comments about the game without participating in it.*

FURTHER READING: *To learn more about the critic, read* Taming Your Gremlin *by Richard Carson, or for a more psychological perspective, read* Embracing Your Inner Critic *by Hal Stone and Sidra Stone.*

Negotiate Your Piece of the Pie

Raises come in many forms. Once upon a time, getting a raise almost always meant getting an increase in base salary; that's the way it was for years and years. Decades, really. If we were given a raise it nearly always came in the form of a salary increase. If you showed up on a fairly regular basis, if you were doing good work and not bugging management too much, you were usually given somewhere around a 4 percent raise every year. That was about average.

Now that **THE RULES HAVE CHANGED,** something different is happening, a direct result of the fundamental change in the way we do business today. Something better for the worker. That *is* different. Companies have had to reinvent themselves. Workers have had to do the same and compensation packages have had to follow suit.

One of the things we're going to examine in this chapter is the way we view traditional forms of compensation. The almighty raise is only one component (and likely not the most important) in the compensation package as it's being offered today. For many people in the workplace today, base salary, while not insignificant by any means, is far from being the most important form of compensation. All of which brings me to one of my favorite subjects: **How you can make more money.**

In olden times, you were considered a good worker and given a raise (and maybe a promotion, though that was rare) if, a) you worked very hard, b) you were a team player, and c) you were on time every day. That's not necessarily the case today.

I have a lot of clients who put in long hours, wear their noses out on the grindstone, go the extra mile, love the companies they work for, and yet don't get big raises or the stock options. Why? Because they haven't positioned themselves correctly, nor have they approached the company in the right way.

First thing you should do is forget the idea that you deserve something because you show up and work hard every day. The company doesn't owe you anything other than an agreed-upon salary, and you'll be better off if you approach the issue with that mind-set. I'm not saying you shouldn't be rewarded for your performance, but you can't harbor the thinking that you deserve it.

I'm sure you all remember the great rallying cry—"Employees are our most important asset." That's probably true as far as it goes; the trouble is, it doesn't go very far. If employees were indeed the most important asset, we wouldn't be seeing the massive layoffs we've seen in the last few years.

Companies, for the most part, want to compensate you in a combination of ways, rather than just on the basis of base salary. The primary focus is going to be pay based on performance—pay based on the value that you bring to the company. In other words, pay based on how much you increase the value of the company. You need to show the company that, as a result of what you're doing, you're adding value—that you're increasing the net worth of the company.

Again, while there will always be a place for the drones and the worker bees, the "infantry" of the workplace, they are the ones who will be locked into three to four percent raises. Moreover, they will be the first ones placed on the waiver wire or released outright in a merger or acquisition, or a downsizing. To get ahead and dramatically improve your salary and compensability, you must think *How can I add value to the company?*

With That in Mind, Here are the Ten Best Ways to Make a Lot More Money:

1. Use a Proposal Format

Anything to do with your compensation, whether it is a promotion, more money, or a piece of the action, needs to be done in a written, businesslike proposal form. Don't wait till you're so angry or worked up about it that you can't talk about or write down your argument. That's not the way to approach any company. First, write up your proposal articulating why you deserve a raise or increased benefits or a promotion. Next, make an appointment with your boss to discuss your employment. The courtesy will be noted and appreciated. Open with a short verbal presentation, then leave your prepared document. Short and to the point. With regard to salary issues, always be proactive.

Approach your boss—don't wait for him or her to approach you. You don't want an automatic raise (as in cost of living, or inflation adjusted) anyway. If you wait for that, you'll have just joined the ranks of those who are getting 3 or 4 percent raises. What you hope for—look for—in a company is flexibility, outside-the-box thinking. A company that likes the fact that you go to them with an idea or proposal that shows how you can add value, how you increase company worth. As a former manager of a sizable company, I can assure you that managers love such approaches to be made in proposal form. They want something they can sit down and evaluate. And they don't want to do so in the heat of an annual review.

2. Compensation Is Negotiable

Compensation is negotiable in almost all companies today, though there are some that still maintain rigid salary structures. The key thing here is to focus more on your position than on the actual dollars. That's what you include in your proposal: here's what my responsibilities are, here is what I would like to do in the future, here is how I'll do it, here is what the work environment will look like, and (most important), *here's how this will benefit the company*. In other words, define what your position will look like as you go forward.

3. Create a Stake in the Outcome

Companies don't respond well to people who clamor for (or demand) more money because they're overworked, understaffed, or underpaid. They prefer employees who come to them and say, "I'd be willing to have a fair amount of my compensation based on, a) how well the company does and, b) how well I do, or how well my team does." The idea here is to demonstrate that you feel strongly enough about your contributions to the company's success that you're willing to stake at least some of your compensation (don't go crazy here—keep it under 30 percent) on the outcome.

Companies love that. They like you to have your skin in the game, too. Sure, there's some risk involved, but there are also big rewards. And of course, the alternative is to stick with those 3 to 4 percent raises every year. If you want to get the 10, 20, and 30 percent raises (yes, they're available), you're going to have to have a stake in the outcome, and take ownership of what's going on.

4. Bonuses

It's now become very common for new employees in certain segments of today's market, such as high-tech or the legal profession, to get a signing bonus. In each of the four job changes I made in the last five years, I got a signing bonus. The least I was given was five thousand dollars, the top was twenty thousand.

Because of the tight labor market, companies use bonuses as a way to attract good people. And it doesn't just apply to top execs anymore. I saw an ad recently for waitstaff in the Denver area that included a signing bonus of a thousand dollars. Nurses in some areas are getting up to five thousand dollars.

Another bonus that is not as well known, but which is now becoming available, is the retention bonus. If you're good at what you do, and the company wants to keep you (this is particularly true in technology), they're often willing to pay you a retention bonus. Though I've seen retention bonuses as high as a full year's salary, most commonly they run to one month's pay.

More obscure yet is the exit bonus. In the case of a merger or acquisition, or if you suddenly find your department's task has been outsourced, you can negotiate an exit bonus of one to two months salary (in addition to your severance pay and whatever else you have coming).

But you must remember to ask for it. Make a request for a bonus part of your proposal that you submit to your employer. It's often negotiable. And it's a way to add more money to your base salary.

5. Be Flexible

You want the company to view you in a different light. If you want to succeed in the marketplace, phrases like "It's not my job," or "I wasn't hired to do that" have no place in your thinking or in your vocabulary. If you're in shipping and receiving you might well be asked to find a more efficient way to ship widgets to Tierra del Fuego. It *is* your job (if you hope to get ahead) to meet new responsibilities, propose changes, get the company to look at you in a different light. When it comes to negotiation time, they're going to see that you're bringing more value to the company, and consequently will be willing to give you a bigger raise.

6. Strategic Job Jumping

Job jumping, once viewed with disdain by the business community, has become a prominent feature in the landscape of today's job market. I was reading an article in the *Denver Post* the other day by a man named James Challenger, a partner in one of the old revered career counseling companies based in Chicago, who said that he felt strategic job jumping was a legitimate strategy. Mr. Challenger is sixty-five years old, has been in career counseling for almost forty years, and I can almost guarantee you that his position was far different only a few years ago. But it's more common now; people on both sides of the bargaining table are recognizing job jumping for what it is: a legitimate career strategy that can benefit both parties. The worker gets the benefit of current market value (or better) for his or her labor. The company hiring the worker gets an additional resource, someone with experience and new ideas.

7. Change Careers

Some of the same principles that apply to strategic job jumping, apply here, too. My own career is a perfect example. When I went from the office products industry to the computer technology industry, I changed careers and got a 40 percent increase in salary. And it was mainly because I had a lot of experience and success selling to corporate America. The computer industry at the time had lots of people who were great at technology, but relatively few people who were great at corporate level sales. A client of mine who was an emergency room nurse changed careers (to sales) and in the first year tripled the amount of money she made in her best year as a nurse. Granted, such a move can be scary, but it can also be very lucrative.

8. Become an Independent Contractor

There's a big trend in the market today for companies to outsource parts of their total operation. And in most cases it's beneficial to both the company and its employees. The company is able to get rid of a lot of peripheral expenses (insurance, office space, cars, etc.), while the employees outsourced can often make a good deal more than they would if they worked directly for the company.

9. Be a Star Performer

Regardless of what you do, be it a nurse, accountant, or receptionist, if you're a star performer you're going to get the big bonuses, the stock options, the right kind of compensation. Remember, good companies will go the extra mile to get and keep the best people. If you're not at least attempting to become one, all bets are off.

10. If You Disagree, Don't Be Disagreeable

Some people attempt to ask for additional compensation through the use of ultimatums. This is a very bad strategy. It will not work, even in a tight labor market. You'll create more ill will than it is worth. I've seen cases where the worker used an ultimatum to get what they wanted in the short term, only to find out they were in a cul-de-sac later when it came to promotions. Trapped. Either way, it's a terrible strategy.

If you disagree with the outcome of your most recent proposal, send a memo to your boss or decision maker thanking him (or her) for the chance to meet and present your ideas about the new position (or new compensation package). And let your boss know that though you were somewhat disappointed in the outcome, you're confident that in time the issue can be resolved in a way that will be mutually beneficial. Most managers will appreciate the fact that you handled the situation professionally.

An option is to test the waters and see what your value is on the open market. Go to Web sites like *salary.com* or *erieri.com*. They will show you what your value is in your industry, in your market. Or go interview with companies who are looking for someone like you to see what they think you are worth. Once determined, you can then approach your boss with the findings. Be professional about it. Tell your boss, "I've been approached by certain people with an offer. I'd rather stay here. Can we get together and see if we can work something out?"

Today's job market is ideal to help you get what you want—if you approach it in the right way. If your goal is to make more money and achieve more balance in your life, you can do that by doing the necessary research and approaching other companies. There were times in the past, the recent past, when it wasn't so easy to move or move up, and the employee was more of a hostage to the system. But the pendulum has swung to the worker's side. Article after article in magazines and newspapers underscore my point: The worker is in a great position to get what he or she wants.

In the second half of this chapter, I want to talk about how to get a piece of the pie. The truth is that many companies are willing to give more equity to more employees. Employers understand that the workforce situation has changed, and the better companies are giving stock options and other inducements to attract and retain people. We're in a very tight labor market, and companies are desperate for skilled employees in many areas. In order to attract and keep the best employees, they have to offer an attractive compensation package.

How to Get a Piece of the Action

Ask for It

The most important thing is that you ask for it. That would seem obvious, but it's not to many people. You'd be surprised at the number of people I talk with who are upset because their company isn't giving them a chance to own stock options in the company. (Stock options are an agreement to buy stock in the company at an agreed upon discounted price. Learn more about how to negotiate stock options by researching *salary.com* or going to the local library.) Most companies are not going to offer such compensation unless you push them for it—unless you ask.

At one time companies were willing to give stock options to only a select few; now they're much more willing to spread the wealth. I know a number of companies that give stock options to almost everyone—janitors, receptionists, vice presidents. Those are also companies who are doing well in the market. Companies like HP, Cisco, and Microsoft.

Coincidence? I don't think so.

Be a Star Performer

What's a star performer? Someone who consistently performs at a level higher than required by that person's boss or their written position description. It's tough to go to your boss and ask for a stock option or for some equity if you are only an average performer. To be a star performer, you have to think like a small-business owner instead of an employee. Consider what you do as your own mini business. If you work hard and find creative ways to do business, you'll prosper. If not, you're just putting in time on the clock. There'll be no action to get a piece of. At least not in your part of the forest.

Go to Work for a Company That Shares the Wealth

When you are first looking for a job, I coach my clients to investigate potential employers to see if they share the wealth. Ask for specific examples of how that works. Ask them what percentage of their employees currently have an equity position. Ask them what the company's plans are for the future. Ask them how flexible and open to negotiation they are. If the responses aren't positive, perhaps that isn't a company you'd want to work for.

What types of equity are available?

A) One is the stock option, the most common form of equity in a company. You're potentially in an exceptionally good position if you go to work for a start-up company. The upside is that you may become a millionaire in a very short time if the company successfully goes public. The downside is that you may work your tail off—sixteen-hour days seven days a week—and end up with a pretty paltry paycheck.

B) Shares in projects. Some companies have discovered that they can't afford to give up more of the company via stock options. In lieu of that, they've developed a method whereby individuals or teams get shares in a new project. Say a company's rolling out a new product or opening a new market or starting a new service; those involved would receive shares contingent upon certain timelines, profitability, and other projections. You'd get shares in the project which you could turn into cash at some predetermined time. Typically, all those details are worked out prior to the start of the project and contained in a written agreement.

C) Phantom shares. Some companies have no intention of going public. Some of these companies have created phantom shares. The employee invests cash in the company and, based upon a predetermined and agreed-upon set of performance metrics, the principle rises or falls, depending on how the company or the project does. There's a buyout provision of course, usually after three to five years. I've known people who have invested a few thousand dollars and walked away four or five years later with a very healthy nest egg. We are talking anywhere from a few thousand dollars to upper six figures.

Companies today realize that giving employees a piece of the action is simply good business. It's a way to motivate people, and to attract and keep the best people available. Learn to position yourself with your employer and get in on the action.

Case Study #1

Maria was a client who worked in inside sales, taking customer calls, tracking orders, dealing with warranty issues. Although she liked the job, she wanted something more challenging and something that paid more money. With a little coaching from me, she went to the decision maker in her company and proposed that she take on a new position whereby she would be the lead on-site person at a major account. The company had a client who was buying millions of dollars of computer products and services; in her proposal she suggested that she work on-site at the customer's facility so she could get a better feel for their needs and requirements. Part of her proposal incorporated programs she had developed which she could implement with the client to help them do a better, more efficient job with ordering products and services.

Her boss loved it and the client loved it. And she got a piece of the action by negotiating a percentage of the increased sales and profits. She ended up making 38 percent more in total compensation for the year.

Case Study #2

Rick was a CPA who had worked in that capacity with several large companies. Unfortunately, he was locked into that mid single-digit raise track, the slow track. We worked together and came up with a strategy that involved looking for a technology start-up company. He hooked up with a small company as the chief financial officer, his highest position to date. Though he actually took a cut in pay, he got a significant piece of the action in the form of stock options, performance bonuses, and the promise that, as the company grew and prospered, his compensation would change to reflect that. At the end of two years he was making more money than ever, plus he had several thousand shares of stock in a software development company that happened to hit it big. He effectively doubled his total compensation over the two years, plus ended up with a solid six-figure nest egg. Of course, not all of us can hit it so big—but the lesson here is that by reevaluating where you are and rethinking what it is you want you can reinvent yourself or your job, and work to land a position with your present company or another company that will give you what you want.

Chapter Seven: Exercises

EXERCISE 1 Evaluate Your Strategies for Increasing Your Compensation

It's not enough to be valuable to your company. You have to be seen to be valuable. A baseball player who hits dramatic, game-winning home runs three times a year will get noticed more than the solid performer who hits .300 and shows up every day. That's America: We are drawn to people who exhibit not just skill, but an innate sense of timing. The following exercises give you some starting points for planning a well-compensated future.

1. Look for home run opportunities

Star performers are always on the lookout for home runs. They find the great opportunities because they continually look for them. They know how to take advantage of an opportunity when they find one.

Go ask your boss what would be a home run for the company. Then ask yourself what you could do to bring it about.

2. Know what you want

How much money do you want to make next year? The year after? Five years from now? Be specific. When you've written your plan, include it in your career map. "As much as possible" is not a useful answer to these questions. You need to have a specific figure in mind, and a plan which will manifest that amount of income. It gives you something concrete to work toward, and a measure of when you have succeeded. If you want to be a millionaire by the time you're forty-five, you'd better have a well-crafted plan which has the potential to take you there. If you just want to be comfortable and debt free by forty-five, it suggests a totally different plan.

COACH'S HINT: *Successful and satisfied people know how much is enough. They know that more isn't always better. They know that jobs which pay the big bucks can have costs too: less time, less freedom, more ulcers. Trust me when I tell you that knowing how much money is enough is one of the key ingredients to a satisfying career (and a satisfying life). At a certain point in your financial life, more money just doesn't translate into a measurably better life.*

PITFALL ALERT:

The desire for more income is often a band-aid solution to poor management of your personal finances. Every financial advisor will tell you that it's not how much you make that counts, it's how much you keep. If you think of increasing your income as the only solution to reaching your financial goals, you're missing a huge factor. Your spending patterns determine your financial well-being as much as your earning patterns. Increasing income when you don't have a handle on your spending is like pouring more water into a bucket with a hole in the bottom.

3. Be willing to ask for what you want

If you don't ask for more, it's guaranteed you won't get it. At some point, you have to ask. Knowing when and how is the trick. Your critic (see Chapter 6) will try and sabotage you by convincing you that it's never quite the right time, or that you're not really worth the salary you're asking for.

Crucial to any negotiation is your genuine confidence that your labor is worth more than you are currently being paid. This doesn't mean you go into a compensation negotiation thinking that you're owed something and feeling resentful about being slighted. *It means you know what you can do, you know what you have done, and the value you have to your business.* Don't let your gremlin diminish your worth, and you're halfway to winning this particular battle.

What does your critic say about asking for more?

What's an alternative way to look at it which would make you likely to put together a strong proposal and negotiate a great compensation package?

4. Research, Part One: What are the compensation potentials of your current career?

Before you position yourself for a more senior job in your current area of expertise, do some research about possible salaries. There are many Web sites which give you access to this information (such as *www.salary.com*). If the top level of your area of expertise earns $85K and your financial plan calls for a six-figure income, you may need to explore other career paths, or find ways to add additional value to that position. If you're going to negotiate a great compensation package, you have to know what's normal for that position, and what's usually included in the job description. If you can add elements to the job description that increase your value to the company, you are in a strong negotiating position.

5. Research, Part Two: Do you know how to negotiate?

Making yourself more valuable to your employer will get you nowhere if you don't know how and when to ask for more. Brush up your negotiating skills. There are plenty of good books in this area, which show you what successful negotiators do. Try your local library, or articles on career sites on the Web.

An investment in building good negotiation skills will repay itself many times over.

6. What kind of compensation do you want?

Answer the following inquiries. *If you have trouble answering these questions, talk them over with a financial advisor.*

- How much of your compensation would you be willing to link to your personal performance?

- How much of your compensation would you be willing to link to the long-term performance of the company (i.e., shares and stock options)?

- What kind of compensation package would most motivate you to perform?

Sometimes, all the negotiation strategies and skills lead nowhere. Sad but true. If you keep coming up against a wall, it might be time to ask yourself **the big question . . .**

Should I Consider a Career Change?

You find yourself peering down a career path that doesn't appear to offer much potential for growth, either financially or personally. It's not fun, it's not moving you forward to your financial goals, your happy meter has stopped working, and you no longer look forward to going to work. Sound familiar? ▷

There are two options here:

1. Assume that the problem is in the job you have or the company you work for.

   The solution: Find a better job in a better company.

2. Assume that your attitude and your choices have something to do with how you experience your job.

   The solution: Reinvent yourself in your current career, using the model of the change agent and star performer.

COACH'S HINT: *Jobs are rather like intimate relationships. Sometimes you're just with the wrong person, it isn't healthy, and it's best for everyone to just end the relationship. Sometimes a relationship is worth working on. All you can do is DO YOUR BEST: Show up with your passion, your gifts, and your commitment, and you'll be surprised how your work environment (and your perception of it) can transform. If it doesn't, you've lost nothing, and had some great practice learning to be a star performer and change agent.*

- Make the commitment to being a star performer in your current job for a predefined period of time (three or six months is a good starting point). Practice your star performer skills diligently, and see what doors open for you which you wouldn't have seen before. If they don't, you can move on to your next job in the secure knowledge that you did your part, and probably with great references, too.

- What is missing in your current position, the presence of which would make your career more fulfilling? *Imagine you could find this in your current job. Where would you look?*

When it's genuinely time for a career change, here are the best two questions to start your search. Take your time with them: They could be the foundations of a new career path.

- What would you do if you knew you could not fail?

- What would you do if money was not a factor in your career choices?

Got the Interview?
Now Get the Job!

If you think there have been a lot of changes in the job market in the last few years, fasten your seat belts because the next five years will see things change even more dramatically. This means that in every area of your career planning you're going to have to rethink your basic strategy about the ways in which your career will grow and prosper.

I can't emphasize enough that even if you are doing well at the moment, if you don't understand what's around the corner you're liable to be blindsided several years down the road. If you think that you have the job market "figured out," you may find yourself in for a rude awakening in the not too distant future. Don't get blindsided because your career strategy is a decade old.

What I want to talk about in this chapter is taking steps to respond to the new job market. Though some companies still require a résumé from prospective employees, résumés are rapidly becoming a thing of the past. What is taking its place is the job proposal. The job proposal has worked for me and many of my clients.

But whether you are evaluated on the basis of a job proposal, a résumé, or an interview, the goal is to differentiate yourself from the other candidates.

Though the job market is tilted in the direction of employees, it is not without competition. In addition to recent grads who are first-time job seekers, there are lots of people *presently employed* who are looking for better positions. So you have to be prepared.

Job Proposals

A job proposal is a very effective tool to get you in front of the person you want to see at the company you want to go to work for. And that's what you want. Résumés are designed to do the same thing; the difference is that nobody's going to hire you on the strength of a résumé, no matter *how* good it is. Employers will still need to see you, to talk to you, to ask questions about how you would respond to certain situations. That is the purpose of the time-honored interview. Both a great résumé and a great job proposal are designed to set you up for the interview. Without getting an interview, you're never going to get hired. ▷

In the past, prospective employees were under the misconception that a great résumé was going to win the job. *Essentially, all résumés do is get you on the list of people to be considered.* When a job posting goes out, companies are usually deluged with résumés. Technology has allowed people across the country to post résumés on job billboard Web sites. Examples of big-name sites include *HeadHunter.net, CareerMag.com, Monster.com, 6figurejobs.com,* and *Techies.com.* The Human Resources department of the hiring manager does key word searches on such electronic résumés, and if you don't have the right key word(s), you are ruled out. You don't even make the first cut. Think about it. For a managerial job, if they get five hundred résumés (which is not unusual), they're going to want to talk to fifteen, twenty, maybe thirty people at most. For a lower level job, they may get twenty to thirty résumés, and only want to talk to five to ten people at most. So the bulk of the work is done to rule people *out*, rather than rule them *in*. I know some terrific people, highly skilled in their area of expertise, people many companies would be glad to have, who get ruled out simply because they don't have the right résumé. If you don't get a call back after you submit your résumé for a job you're sure you are perfect for, the reason is that you haven't done a good job differentiating yourself from the competition on your résumé. My point is not to bash résumés—they have their place; I have to drive home the fact that you want to differentiate yourself from the rest of the people seeking the job you want. And that is the purpose of the job proposal.

Just what is a job proposal? It is a one- or two-page mini business plan that you present to the company in order to get an interview. How you go about presenting this material is markedly different from a résumé. A résumé primarily tells what you've done in the past; a job proposal tells what you're *going* to do in the job you're applying for when you get it. Then, when you get into the interview situation and the company wants to clarify some of the ways in which you've told them you can help them, your track record comes into play—you can show them how the skills you have developed during your previous experience meshes well with what they're trying to accomplish.

In the job proposal, you want to be as specific as you can be about what you're going to do for the company to whom you are applying for a job. The proposal tells the company you're interested enough to find out what they do, how they do it, where they're strong and perhaps where they're not so strong. It shows them you're a problem solver, an independent thinker, someone who has thought through the requirements of the job and has a game plan to get the job done.

Again, when I made four job changes in five years, receiving the signing bonuses and the stock options and tripling my pay, I used a job proposal. And though the companies may not have hired me to implement exactly the ideas I spelled out in my proposal, it showed I had thought through the job and its requirements—and it differentiated me from the rest of the field. The companies liked the fact that I was creative enough to come up with some new ideas that might help them, *even if the ideas themselves were not a perfect fit.*

You should include in your job proposal exactly what you're going to do for the company (to the best of your knowledge), including your responsibilities, other team members you'd like to see be a part of this enterprise, three or four main things you hope to accomplish, and the time frame you anticipate to get them done.

You might even propose opening a new office for them. I did this with Entex, who, at that time, didn't have a presence in the Denver area. I found out who the key decision maker was and presented my two-page mini business plan. In it, I proposed to open a new office for them here in Denver, explaining what my title would be, what team members I would require for a successful operation, how we would go after the market, and the kinds of accounts we would target, among other things.

Whether you are applying for a managerial job or a job as a legal secretary, the job proposal shows that you've done your research, you've talked to some people in the company, or someone who knows how the company operates. You probably won't get anybody to give you inside information—you don't need it and probably don't want it anyway—but you can get valuable insights into how the company operates and what direction they're taking or intend to take.

The job proposal should be very businesslike; the language you use should reflect that. You want to quickly and succinctly get to the key elements in your proposal.

Once you've finished the job proposal, send it to the decision maker for the particular position that you're applying for. How do you find that out? Make inquiries—do your research. What you don't want to do is send your proposal through ordinary channels like Human Resources or the Employment Office. Your chances of being noticed are going to be greatly reduced. So find the decision maker, find out how they like to receive communication (fax, snail mail, e-mail), and send it. The information about how people like to receive communications is not all that hard to find out. You can call the receptionist at the targeted company and explain that you're sending some material to Mr. Smith and were wondering how he likes to receive his communication. If the person doesn't know, he or she will send you back to the department in question and you'll get an answer closer to the source. I have never not been able to find out (is that a double negative?).

The job proposal is the current (and future) vehicle to use to get you noticed and to differentiate you from the competition. Not many people use the job proposal right now. A number of my clients have used it over the last year and our success ratio is two to three times what we get just using the straight résumé. It's part of the new thinking. It's a new way of looking at how you have thought through and developed your career as well as how you work to get where you want to go (see "Career Mapping," Chapter 4). I can say unequivocally that it works. Use it.

Résumés

I want to spend a little time on the résumé itself because they're still the coin of the realm with some companies. I'm not saying they never work, because sometimes they *do* work, and in some cases it's the only legal tender a company will accept. So, although fewer and fewer companies require it, it's probably best to have an updated résumé available.

Today's companies are looking for creative thinkers, problem solvers, change agents, people who are, above all, flexible and willing to take on new roles as needed to help the company succeed. So your résumé should reflect that attitude. It should be accomplishment oriented rather than just a list, chronologically arranged, of whom you worked for and a brief description of what you did while you were there. What companies want today are people who get stuff done. Those are the people who can point to measurable achievements, who can talk about specific accomplishments. Employers want to see what you've done in the jobs you've held, not what positions you've held or companies you've worked for (although you certainly want to put that in).

Your résumé should be one page long. That's all. Nobody is going to sit around and read three- or four-page résumés. Do away with all the flowery exposition and get to the accomplishments. List your six or eight top achievements; where possible have them be measurable achievements, expressed in percentages, numbers, results. Maybe it's the percentage you reduced accounts receivable by, or how you handled customer problems on the first call instead of the second or third, or how much your sales increased in a specified period. Doesn't make any difference if you're a receptionist or a truck driver; list your accomplishments.

What I *don't* like to see is the opening gambit that goes *here's my goal, here's my objective, I want to get with a great company so I can maximize my skills.* Get rid of that stuff. They know that already. Cut right to the chase. If need be, put that in a short cover letter, but don't waste the space on your résumé.

Since you still need to list the where and when in your employment record, I suggest that, rather than taking up nearly the entire résumé (as it usually does), it take up only a quarter of it. (See pages 133–34 for a sample résumé.) What you'll see is a very concise synopsis, a single-line listing, e.g.:

1990–1994: Systems engineer for Hewlett-Packard.

1995–1999: Technical Analyst for Microsoft.

Or 1989–1999: Marketing Manager, Procter & Gamble

Don't list what you did, what your responsibilities were; companies want to know about accomplishments and achievements, not responsibilities. Another point is to list relevant education, and (perhaps as important today) computer or technology skills. There are very few jobs today that don't require some degree of computer literacy.

You won't have to be able to write a software program, but even if you're a waiter or waitress, you should be informed enough to do simple keyboard entry. So list such skills—and more is better in this case.

While résumés will continue to play a role in the twenty-first century, their importance will diminish. The point I want to make is that if you're using the résumé as your primary tool to get your foot in the door and win an interview, you're probably going to be disappointed. I have had clients come to me with stories about having sent out fifty or a hundred résumés and getting no, repeat *no*, response. The reason, again, is that résumés are used to weed people *out*, not get them in. If you want to be ruled in and differentiate yourself from your competitors, think job proposal.

Interviews

Preparing for an interview is vital. After going to all the trouble to prepare a job proposal, or a combination of a job proposal and a résumé, just to land an interview, you want to be sure you're prepared.

First, dress the part. Obviously you should look your best when going to a job interview. It's not as important to get dressed in a stylish business dress or suit as it once was (to the disappointment of Brooks Brothers and Ann Taylor), but don't dress too casually, either.

Second, be passionate about the company and the job. The last thing any company is looking for is another body to take up space. I'm sure they've got their quota of those. They want people who are doers, who have accomplished things, who are eager, enthusiastic, creative self-starters. Don't be afraid to let it show. I've interviewed literally thousands of people and remarkably few seem to display the kind of passion that most companies get excited about. I've short-listed people for return interviews who didn't have qualifications equal to some other candidates solely because of their enthusiasm. When I saw several candidates with the proper background and skills and qualifications, the deciding factor for me was always passion about the job. You don't have to dance on the desktop and strike up the chorus to "Singin' in the Rain," but don't be afraid to display the fact that you are excited about their product or service or to tell why you think you'd be a great fit. And if you're not enthusiastic about the company and the job, that should serve as a notice to you that you shouldn't even be going on the interview.

One of the ways you can show your enthusiasm or passion is the way you sit in your chair during the interview. Don't sit back with your arms crossed; that's a "show me" stance. It conveys a bad message. Be confident, polished, and professional. Being "cool" went out around the time that *Happy Days* went into reruns.

Bring with you any information that supports the position you're taking. If you've presented a job proposal that entails a new responsibility or task, you want to bring with you all the documentation you have that backs your position. It will establish your credibility and the validity of your proposal. It says that you're an organized person, that you've done your research, that you walk the walk.

Bring with you to the interview any awards or commendations that you've received. I've actually pulled plaques and what have you out of my briefcase to show at interviews. They are visible evidence of accomplishments. Companies like people who can accomplish things. And it has differentiated me from the competition.

The questions you ask of the person interviewing you also say a lot about who you are. I coach my clients to try to—diplomatically of course—take control of the interview. The sooner the better. Don't ask what the company is going to do for you. Instead, tell the interviewer what you're going to do for the company. And after your presentation or proposal, ask key questions based on the research you did. It will distinguish you from the competition and help you decide if this is a company you really want to work for. Here are some legitimate questions you should want to know the answers to:

How would you describe your company's management style?

What's the company's management philosophy?

How do you help employees balance their professional and personal lives?

What will my specific job responsibilities be?

What will I be expected to accomplish in the few months or the first year?

How would you describe the company culture?

What kind of people are most satisfied working for you?

What is the staff turnover ratio?

Why do you think people leave here?

What are the company's values?

How will my work be evaluated?

Is there room for growth and advancement in the company? Ask for specific examples.

What is the company doing for continuing education and training?

How is the company positioned against the competition?

How does the company keep employees apprised of new developments?

If the interviewer has a hard time answering your questions or is vague in his or her response, that's a warning flag. It should make you wonder if this is the kind of company you want to work for.

Let's say you've had a great interview, you like the company and you think the feeling's mutual. What's the next step? When is it okay to contact the company? That, in fact, is one of the questions you might ask to end the interview. What's the next step? What's the timeline?

I recommend to my clients that they send an e-mail or fax in the next couple of days, not only thanking their interviewer for their time, but perhaps bringing out a point or two that you wanted to discuss but didn't get around to.

When do you bring up the issue of compensation? I always save it until the end, after I've decided that this is the company for me.

And the way to bring it up is simply to say something like, "Do you mind if we take a few minutes and talk about compensation?" Simple and effective. Make the point that you're talking about total compensation, not just base salary or hourly wage. Let them know what you expect, what your research indicates is the going rate, plus anything extra (signing bonus, etc.) that you'd like included in the offer.

The company likes to think that it's not *just* money that brings you to the party. That doesn't mean you're not going to negotiate to get what you want, because you are. They know that. But if you've set the tone by describing your accomplishments and skills and asking the great questions, you're going to end up getting more money. Just keep it in the proper sequence.

Bottom line? Great job proposals win great interviews; great interviews win the great jobs. You want to write a real winner of a proposal to get considered, but you have to nail the interview to get the job. Remember that the winning interview is not based on your Armani suit or the fact that you just bought shares in the company. Winning the job is about having an idea of how your employment will benefit the company, presenting your case with passion and enthusiasm. Demonstrate that you're a problem solver, a creative thinker, a change agent, and the job will be yours.

Chapter Eight: Exercises

THE JOB PROPOSAL

By now, you know why job proposals get interviews, and résumés find their way into landfills. The only way to get good at job proposals is to practice. Your mission, should you choose to accept it, is to write at least **three** job proposals. Your goal is to reach the following stages with each proposal:

1. Practice your proposal skills on a job you currently have (or your most recent job), and learn the differences between writing a résumé and writing a proposal.

2. Begin to exercise your research muscles. Complile a proposal for a company you'd like to work for. Choose a company where you have an inside contact.

3. Complete a proposal, which contains all of the required elements listed below, is sharply presented, and present it to your target inside the company.

Required Elements of a Job Proposal

Here's a list of the elements you should include in a job proposal. Always remember that, unlike résumés, job proposals are written to speak to the needs and interests of a specific person within a specific company. It should be a maximum of two pages.

1. Core proposal
Summarize your proposal. Tell the reader what they're about to read.
You might try a catchy title, like a newspaper headline.

2. Your company's need
Thoroughly researched, specific, and verified by your inside contacts.

3. My solution
Concrete, direct, focused, and measurable.

4. My skills
Pick your top five.

COACH'S HINT: *Focus on those skills which are outstanding, set you apart, and will be visible to others.*

5. My impact on a business
How is a business environment, team, or community different because you're a part of it? What do you bring to that community which enhances the performance and fulfillment of those within it?

6. What sets me apart from others who are similarly qualified

Don't brag, *distinguish*. What's normal for people in your role? What will you bring to the position which will make you a star performer?

7. Invitation to action

What action would you like the prospective employer to take after they've read your proposal?

Optional Elements

Include only those that strengthen and add to your central point. More is not necessarily better in these proposals.

What excites me about the prospect of working for your company

One idea is to speak to the company's mission statement.

Who am I

An opportunity to say who you choose to be as an employee, not what box you fit in.

What I have done in the past

Past achievement highlights, successes, wins. Highlight any home runs you've hit which are related to the substance of this proposal.

What I *will* do in the future

This is where you say what you have chosen as your future. Focus on results for the company, not for you.

30/60/90/180 days (specific, measurable results)

This is how that future will manifest in your business, broken down into developmental stages.

I will consider this a success if . . .

Build in some measurability, show that you're willing to think big, and you know what it'll take to get there.

What I will need to succeed

Not the place to ask for a certain salary (that comes much later), but the place to describe the support, attitudes, environment, and business philosophy that will bring out the best in you.

My mission

What do you stand for? What is your professional life really about? What is the compelling reason for you to participate in this kind of work? What gets you out of bed in the morning feeling positive about your day?

My vision

How can you bring your mission down to earth, into daily practice, and use it as a foundation from which to build an action plan? What is your vision for the department you will lead?

My commitment

What is nonnegotiable. What you will stand for, whether others agree or disagree. What qualities of being and modes of operation will be ever present.

My network

Where are you connected? What is your community? Who do you know? Who do you naturally relate to? (and how these will relate to the success of your proposal).

You can hold me accountable for . . . (My guarantee)

Guarantees are powerful. What would you be willing to guarantee absolutely, with your job on the line?

What moves, touches, and inspires me about this opportunity

Speak from the heart: Be totally authentic. This is where you get to say that this will be more than just a job.

Top ten reasons to hire me

Be specific, but you can be playful, too, since top ten lists are supposed to be funny.

My business philosophy

Avoid clichés, focus on concrete statements of intent, your boundaries, your ethics, what you believe in and stand for.

What my colleagues/supervisors/clients have said about me

Direct quotes and testimonial, with references and follow-up phone numbers.

Refining and Delivering Your Proposal

It has been said that anyone can write, but only a gifted few can rewrite well. The first draft of your job proposal needs feedback and then revision. Here's a sequence of events.

1. You've done your homework, and you know what you want to propose to whom. Not only is it a great idea on a practical, business level, it also excites you, speaks to an area of passionate interest.

2. You have an inside coach who confirms that the idea is sound, and guides you about how to present it, and to whom.

3. You write the proposal. Show it to at least two people for feedback. Tell them your intended audience, and ask them to evaluate it from that perspective. Based on their feedback, rewrite if necessary.

4. Show your proposal to your inside coach. Rewrite it again, as required. It should now fit the two-page requirement. Check that it not only conveys your proposal effectively, but it has a flavor of your personality and style about it.

5. Mail or hand-deliver your proposal. HAND DELIVERY IS THE PREFERRED METHOD. If you mail it, I suggest FedEx or UPS, because they allow you to

go on-line and track the exact moment when your proposal was delivered (see #6 below for why this is important).

6. On the day your target will be receiving your proposal, leave them a brief message (thirty seconds max) early that morning saying that they'll be receiving a proposal from you today, and letting them know when you'll follow up. (When they do get it that day, you've shown that you can deliver what you promise. Simple but impressive.)

7. Follow up within forty-eight hours of their receipt, at the exact time you said. Don't ask for a response right away on the phone, ask for a meeting to discuss your proposal. Always call it a meeting rather than an interview.

JOB PROPOSAL
To: Colorado College of Chiropractic
From: Paul Wyman, CPPC
June 7th, 2000

The intent of this document is to give you a sense of the kind of energy and ideas I will bring to the position of Director of Admissions.

My résumé gives you a sense of what I've done in the past, but it does not tell you what I will do when hired to work for the Colorado College of Chiropractic.

This is a demonstration of my thought process, business philosophy, and proactive leadership style.

A Vision for the Admissions Department

- Create an admissions department which is vital, lively, and welcoming. Every applicant's dream of becoming a Chiropractic Physician is *celebrated* by staff.

- Recruit and enroll those students who will best represent the philosophy, goals, and character of the Chiropractic profession, and the Colorado College of Chiropractic.

- Provide the academic staff with students who are ready to learn, whose expectations are high but realistic, who are committed to success, and are fully prepared to take on the challenge of becoming an outstanding Chiropractic Physician.

- Institute organizational systems and management practices within the Admissions Department which empowers all department members to perform at a high level.

- Design the department around the organizing principles of **simplicity** and **directness,** in order that all admissions personnel are empowered to work at peak efficiency.

- Design and implement administrative and interdepartmental communication systems which simplify rather than obstruct the delivery of necessary admissions data to college administration.

- Work in a way that is consistent with the philosophy of Chiropractic: for each member of the Admissions team to take responsibility for the "health" of the department, and to strive to create an office which is not just free of overt problems, but is vibrantly healthy.

- Create a department which treats all inquiries and applications with such respect that it naturally generates a flow of referrals from the community. Referrers will know, without a shadow of a doubt, that applicants to CCC will be treated well, will never be pressured, and will be thoroughly and effectively introduced to the college and the profession.

Leadership and Management Style
My approach to the challenge of directing a department that is the first point of contact between the students and the college.

- **Open-door policy:** Available to support the personal and professional development of department staff, open communication, and an atmosphere of trust and mutual support.

- **Manager as Coach:** To look at every breakdown in department functions as an opportunity to generate a breakthrough.

- **Manager as Listener:** To call forth the creativity and passion of each individual, by encouraging full self-expression, open communication, an atmosphere of team participation and nonjudgment.

- **Relentlessly Positive:** Committed to looking for win-win-win solutions to challenges (to be a win for college, department member, and applicant).

- **Accountability:** Where possible, give each department team member choices about how to perform their job, but hold solid accountability to produce bottom line results.

- **Inspiration:** To lead by *inspiring* others to outstanding performance rather than simply requesting it. To inspire by modeling the kind of actions and communication which produce results, and create a positive work environment and team energy.

- **A Culture of Resolution:** Problems in the department do not hang around, unresolved, generating tension, stress, resentment, and high turnover, all of which will negatively impact the recruitment and enrollment process. As Director of Admissions, I will use my extensive conflict resolution skills to do whatever it takes to resolve the problem quickly, in a way that is a win-win for all involved.

- **Celebration and Reward:** Individual and team achievements are celebrated and acknowledged, and where possible, rewarded. All team members know that their hard work is seen, valued, and recognized, and that they are appreciated, regularly and specifically.

Proposed Public Relations and Enrollment Strategies
A little brainstorming about ways to generate ongoing, successful recruitment.

- Gain visibility to target market, through health fairs, college recruitment fairs, informational evenings, and inspirational talks.

- Create P.R. campaign to get extensive local and trade media coverage of college opening.

- Network with my career advisors in the Rocky Mountain Region, generate awareness of the College, its target student profile. Create and nurture relationships with key individuals at "feeder" institutions, including University of Colorado, Colorado State University, University of Northern Colorado, Metro State, Regis, and the many vocational schools in the region.

- Produce outstanding written marketing materials, which both inspire and educate prospective students. Combine to form a packet to be mailed to prospective students that is classy, professional, thorough, personal, and highly informative. The packet should be a step above anything being offered by competitors.

- Create a comprehensive strategy to drive traffic to the college Web site, through Internet banner advertising and business alliances with Web sites which draw our target demographic.

- Create a visible and dynamic presence among Denver area Chiropractors, through networking events, social gatherings, and sponsorship (and perhaps subsidy) of continuing education trainings which are at the leading edge of the profession.

- Highly targeted advertising in print media which is read by our target demographic.

- Create strategic alliances with college-focused career counseling organizations and Web sites, to ensure that Chiropractic careers are included in the thought process of medically inclined college students.

- Design a tour program for students visiting the campus which is managed by Admissions staff, but is led by current students. The goal would be to allow visitors to observe classrooms and labs, get into conversation with present students, and experience the feeling of the campus Chiropractic community. This will involve creating a comprehensive training program for current students to successfully welcome and guide visitors, and emphasize the selling points of the college.

- Generate a referral incentive program for current students and alumni/ae.

Top Ten Reasons to Hire Paul Wyman as Director of Admissions

1. He's creative, resourceful, innovative, *and* practical.

2. He gives outstanding presentations, inspirational talks, and excellent training.

3. He has extensive knowledge and experience in the alternative health care field, and knows the Chiropractic profession extremely well.

4. He's a capable administrator, able to maintain simplicity and effectiveness.

5. He's accountable, responsible, and responsive, a true team player.

6. He has an existing network of contacts in the Chiropractic and alternative health communities in Denver.

7. He is a skilled manager, trainer, educator, and coach.

8. His passion, dedication, and enthusiasm in his work are magnetic. He's a natural recruiter.

9. He has a great English accent!

10. Paul is fun to work with, able to make any workplace more energized, and productive.

I am available for interview from June 12 onward, and for employment from July 1. Please contact me at (303) 795–0744, or through e-mail: Paul.Wyman@Mindspring.com

Delta Road Job Proposal

Proposal

Internet Marketing Coordinator

Objectives

This position would keep track of various marketing functions that Delta Road will encounter in order to stay strategically marketed with a presence on the Internet.

The status of this task will be research intensive, require marketing skill applications, and the ability to maintain functionality of company documents related to the Internet.

General Assumptions

- Our target market will come from the data that we receive from Face-Time. From this I would like to create a target market profile that I will then research on-line to investigate what would best attract them to our site.

- Most of the following processes will have to be perpetually and diligently maintained since the Web is a dynamic and ever-changing environment. Competitiveness and presence on the Internet is a never-ending process because of the quick growth and popularity of the Internet.

Process

Web site search engine registration

Maintaining the registration of the dotcom site to search engines will be of the utmost importance. Also, overseeing the process of registration of the coach sites to search engines will be routinely maintained.

Key word generation and maintenance for main site and coach sites

Knowledge of what key words are being used at search engines and which ones are no longer being used will be helpful in maintaining our functionality and searchability on search engines.

Maintaining and researching technical articles for coaches
Technical articles will be updated every month as needed by the coaches in order to make them feel more comfortable dealing with people who are in high-tech positions. Articles pertaining to other professions can also be added if needed.

Maintaining the technical dictionary
Updates of the technical dictionary available every month as needed by the coaches. Definitions that become of importance could be directly e-mailed to me for updating in the dictionary and definitions that are found through research and deemed with value as a source for the coaches will also be added.

Researching banner ads
The importance of banner ads as a means of advertising on the Web will be important as Delta Road makes their presence known on the Internet. Knowing current information on what is working and what is not will be key to our success with this form of medium. All areas of this subject will be researched, such as color schemes, tag lines, font type, movement, and sites that have had success with them. Continued research on what types of Web ads are working and experiencing the highest clickability rates will also be important and will allow Delta Road to be one of the forerunners to the latest marketing strategies on the Internet.

Researching Internet positioning for Web sites
Positioning is important because Delta Road will want to be in areas on the Internet that their target market is focused on. Finding sites to position Delta Road will be helpful in expanding our presence and will complement our branding efforts.

Researching potential strategic alliances
Finding key strategic alliances will allow Delta Road to develop partnerships with other businesses that will enhance our presence on the Internet. Placement on a strategic alliance's Web site may potentially help with our ratings on search engine sites that rate their searches by popularity.

Maintaining a list of our strategic alliances
This will be an up-to-date list so that everyone in Delta Road will know whom we have strategic alliances with. By maintaining this list it will allow a master list to be in one place with all of the information so everyone will have the same information if they need it.

Internet research
This will allow for extra Internet strategy research to be conducted if and when needed for the Internet strategy team, especially pertaining to Internet marketing strategies.

F u t u r e

Trade Show research

Researching and developing new and innovative ideas for trade show hooks that will get Delta Road noticed and remembered by the public.

Creation and maintenance of college and university strategic alliances

Researching and creating a list of potential alliances with universities and colleges. Potentially developing a pilot program in order to receive feedback and data on this possible alliance.

Creating a buzz on-line

This would allow Delta Road an initial mystique that would create curiosity that would need to be satisfied by potential consumers who would hear/read the words "Delta Road" and would like to find out more.

Keeping abreast of our competitors

Knowing what our competitors are offering will allow us to keep our products and services up to par and potentially excel in what we at Delta Road can offer to our clients and potential clients. This will also allow us to know our standing amongst our competitors and it may potentially allow us to see what is in the minds of our clients and potential clients.

Researching more about our target markets

Target markets will help Delta Road learn about the types of people that use our services. By researching this subject further we will be able to create advertisements in the way of banner ads and/or popup ads that would appeal to them and encourage our target market to click on the advertisement. Knowledge about what our target markets want is the key to finding out what they want to see or what products or services they want access to. Also keeping abreast with our target market will be the key to Delta Road's success in drawing them to our site.

Cost and Timing

- The current rate is $13.00 for part-time contract work up until the point that I am able to work full-time. The proposed rate is $40,000 annually based on research that I conducted looking for similar position compensation and first-year college graduates. Delta Road will reimburse me for materials and supplies that are directly consumed by the company, such as printer ink and paper. Delta Road will be billed monthly.

- After I graduate, which is tentatively mid-August 2000, I would like to increase my hours from 15–20 to 40+. This transition will increase over the period of 3 weeks at 10 hours per week until it is up to 40 hours per week.

- Since I would be working a standard work week, I would like to move to a full-time position and W2 status and away from 1099 Contractor status.

- The estimated time for all of the above to be completed will be now through August and possibly beyond.

Chris Horning
12187 W. Coal Mine Drive, Littleton, Colorado 80127; (303) 987–3655

Summary

Eight-year track record of exceeding sales quotas in the PC systems integration industry. Extensive experience in the sale of technical services and products to the commercial IT market. Proven history of new business development. Comprehensive, consultative selling and project management experience in information technology planning, design, implementation, and support projects.

Selected skills and achievements

- Project lead for a major hardware and software conversion project at US West, Local Markets division in 1996. Developed and implemented a comprehensive project proposal, scope-of-work, and project plan. Managed a team of 7 systems engineers at US West locations throughout the west and mid-western U.S.

- Outsourced and managed a team of eight project engineers at Nextel Communications and generated product revenues of $4 million in 1994.

- Attained the #1 ranking in quota attainment (254%) of a total of 83 sales reps at MicroAge, Inc. in 1994.

- Managed an $8 million hardware and software logistics project at Tele-Communications, Inc.'s Head-end-in-the-Sky, Digital Cable Television roll-out throughout the United States in 1997. In addition, acted as project lead for the coordination of field service resources to over 900 domestic TCI locations.

- Led a team of 6 sales representatives covering the Denver market at MicroAge, Inc. Increased annual sales revenue from $4.2 million in 1990 to over $12 million in 1992. Responsible for all activities including recruitment, training, business development, and attaining financial plans.

- Won the Boston Chicken and Oppenheimer accounts and generated over $4 million in product and services outsourcing business for ENTEX during the last 6 months of 1995.

- Recognized as the #2 Rep in the Central Region for new business development in 4th quarter 1995 while at ENTEX Information Services.

- Extensive knowledge of the Denver commercial IT market including major companies and key contacts.

Employment History

NovaQuest Infosystems, Denver, Sr. Account Executive, 1998–Present
ENTEX Information Services, Denver, Sr. Account Executive, 1995–1998
EnPointe Technologies, Denver, Sr. Account Executive, 1996–1997
MicroAge, Inc., Denver, Sr. Account Manager, 1993–1995; Sales Manager 1990–1993

Education

Metropolitan State College, Denver, Colorado (1974–1978, present)

- 20 credit hours from a B.S. in Mechanical Engineering
- Currently working toward completion

Ask for More ... You'll Probably Get It

Another way that you'll find the workplace has changed is the way workers relate to their bosses. Though there are still old-line bosses out there, and a great many employees who *think* there are still old-line bosses out there (and the way that the relationship between employee and employer remains the way it's always been), in truth the relationship *has* changed. And in the better companies, bosses are changing with the times. What that means is that we now have new opportunities to not only remake our careers and move them forward, but also tend to have a more enjoyable relationship with the people we work for.

Why Ask for More?

When I first got into the job market thirty odd years ago, there was a very linear relationship between employer and employee. I had no trouble understanding where I was on the food chain (think bottom). Nobody ever questioned his or her boss. You were certainly free to not like it or disagree (quietly), but the one thing you were not allowed to do was ignore it. To question your boss's authority was to put your job or career at considerable risk. You could be fired on a mere whim. It was that simple.

While there are still a few power-trippers out there, their numbers are dwindling. If you work for one, I'd suggest you consider moving to pastures that are a little greener; perhaps your career would blossom in different surroundings. If you're interviewing with a new company, make a solid effort to find out what the management style is, what the corporate culture is like before committing to employment.

All that said, the title of this chapter is another indicator of how much the job market has changed. Bosses today, the good ones at least, want you to be bringing more of everything to the table. They're not distressed that you're asking for more because they know you're bringing more. You're not going to show up at your evaluation with a begging bowl in your hand; you're going to show up with a satchel full of ideas and recommendations that will help the company.

Now that the pendulum has swung to our side, the old employment contract is quickly becoming a thing of the past, and the new employment contract is now being written. The primary driver behind the new employment contract is that companies, the good ones, realize that attracting and retaining the best workers is the number-one workplace issue. Supply and demand, folks. There just ain't enough good ones to go around. How many pitchers now throwing in the big leagues would have been in Double or Triple A fifteen years ago? Easy answer: lots. There are a lot more teams, and yet the talent pool remains roughly the same. Look at the number-four and -five starters on most major league rosters; those were the minor leaguers of ten, fifteen years ago.

For years and years the big issue among companies was capital; finding enough money to stay afloat. Today, the big issue is finding and keeping great employees. There are twenty-eight million *less* Gen-xers than Baby Boomers, and when we (the Boomers) start moving out of the job market, well . . . you do the math. You won't even need your calculator. Not enough folks to fill the positions.

What to Ask for

Now that the time is right and the pendulum has swung over to our side, chances are good that if you ask for more you're probably going to get it. All of this presupposes that you're a solid performer. You don't have to be a star (but of course that helps), but you do have to be a solid performer, a real contributor. If you're a so-so (read: mediocre) performer, you're not going to get much consideration.

#1.

You can ask for more money. Very legitimate. My suggestion would be that you not only ask for an increase in your base salary but that you also get a stake in the outcome; i.e., if you exceed certain target figures, you be given a bonus or a percentage of the increase.

#2.

You can ask for more time off, or flextime, as it's come to be known. With telecommuting more of a reality, flextime is just that—the flexibility to work hours that allow you to, say, go to the dentist in the afternoon, maybe attend your kid's soccer game, then complete your daily tasks later in the evening after the kids have gone to bed. You're not so stressed about how you're going to make certain appointments, your work/life balance meter is idling contentedly at mid-scale, and yet all the work gets done.

Sometimes, having the flexibility to telecommute, raise a family, spend more time with the kids, etc., is far more important than the actual dollars you accumulate.

#3.

Ask for more say in company decisions. The best companies allow (nay, encourage) their employees to be more active in company decisions. Maybe not the big BIG ones (they won't ask you about prospective mergers), but decisions on new products, decisions about advertising campaigns, decisions about better ways to get things done, on how to work more effectively as a team. Go to your boss and ask to be involved in some of the company decisions. Maybe you can sit down together and find out which ones you think are appropriate and which are not. If you do that in a professional, diplomatic way, what employer or manager worth his or her salt isn't going to love you? Who doesn't want to shift some of the responsibility to someone who's willing (or eager) to become more involved in company decisions?

#4.

Ask for more assignments. I talked a little about this when I discussed being a star performer. Don't wait for someone to come to you with a task; be proactive. Ask if there's an assignment you can take on. I guarantee you that there will be. Better yet, you can sometimes suggest that some things need to be done which aren't presently getting any attention, and which, perhaps you, being the solid, or star performer that you are, could take care of.

#5.

Ask to share in the company's wealth. This was covered at some length in the previous chapter. Remember that you have to ask for stock options, a piece of the action. You'll also have to have the achievements to show the company that you deserve it.

#6.

These last two may be a little obscure, but I've had some success with them. Tell your boss you want to have more fun. That's right, *f-u-n*. As weird as it sounds, it can be effective. One of the things that makes people want to come to work for a company and stay there is having fun on the job. And oddly enough, if you're having more fun, you're being more productive. So if you've got some ideas about how to make the workplace more fun, take them to the boss. It might involve more interesting assignments, more business travel, the opportunity to work more closely with clients outside the company, etc.

I once had a bunch of people who worked for me. One day we sat down and decided that we ought to have a recess every afternoon. You remember recess? Of course you do. Every afternoon at three we'd go outside and maybe throw the football around, play hacky-sack, float the Frisbee across the lawn. And instead of the three P.M. swan song which most of us went through, we'd look forward to going outside and getting the blood flowing a little (oxygenate those brain cells, gang).

#7.

Ask for a sense of purpose. People today in the workforce want to have a sense of purpose within the company. They want to feel that they make a difference, that they're contributing something of value. They're not sure how to get it, and they may even feel that their values are at cross-purposes with the companies. But it's something to ask for. Ask your employer how you can achieve more of a sense of purpose on the job, how you can come away feeling that you're more than just a body who shows up to get a paycheck.

When to Ask for More

Like all things in life, timing is absolutely paramount in asking your boss for more. One of the things I noticed while toiling away in corporate America was that people weren't achieving their full potential and taking it to the next level because most didn't know how to ask for more, and the few that did, didn't know *when* to ask. There are certain times that such requests are more effective than others.

#1

You can ask during an informational interview (this is the ultimate early warning system). Translation: When you've listed a company that you're considering going to work for, set up an informational interview so you can find out about the company's direction, its vision for the future. During the interview, you can ask about the company culture, about how employees gain a greater sense of purpose, how the company feels about flextime, etc. It's a great time to size up the company, and if you do go to work for them, you'll already have done some groundwork.

#2

Ask at scheduled times. This is very important. But don't wait for the proverbial annual review, or the six-month review. I coach my clients to ask for a ten-minute meeting (sometimes every week, or at the least once a month) outside the normal review process, just to ask how they're doing, and what could they be doing better. It's also a time to ask for more. Of course the outcome will be driven by your performance and what's going on at the company, but do the asking at scheduled times.

#3

Any time your life undergoes a major change is also a time to ask for more from your employer—if you've come back to work after being a stay-at-home mom (that's right, even then), or if you've moved and your commute has increased. Remember to be professional, straightforward, and to ask in a diplomatic fashion. Putting together a proposal is the best way to get what you want, preferably—and most effectively—a verbal proposal followed by a written one. If you find yourself in need of a different kind of structure to achieve the work/life balance that you want and that will consequently improve your work performance, don't be afraid to ask.

#4

Ask when someone else in the company gets more. This can be a little tricky; you can't go whining to the boss every time Sally or Johnny gets a new laptop. That's not going to work. But you should take advantage of the opportunity because the goodies handed out to Johnny or Sally may indicate that the company is in a position to be generous. When you find out that a fellow employee just got a promotion, a raise, or more benefits, that's the time to start planning your own strategy. Timing is everything, so don't approach your boss the next day (or even the next week); wait at least thirty days before you ask. When you do ask, it's OK to say you are aware that new hires or existing employees are receiving raises and new perks. You are simply asking to stay current with those offerings. The key here is not to "demand" anything, but explain how your performance justifies the new rates.

#5

Ask when you have a great idea. Keep in mind that great ideas focus on how to improve things, how to streamline processes, or how the company can make more money. Don't try to blackmail your boss by telling him you're willing to share your great idea if the company is willing to bend to your demands. This, for obvious reasons, is a very bad approach. You won't have an edge on the company; you'll simply short-circuit your career. Share your idea with your boss. If she implements it and it's beneficial to the company, *then* you will have enough leverage to ask for more.

#6

Ask for more if you're a star performer. Stars in other fields (entertainment, sports) always request, and generally get, perks and raises after a blockbuster performance. It's also true in the workplace. If you've had a great year, even a great quarter, that's when you make your move. And always remember to operate with diplomacy and a professional attitude.

How to Ask for More

A businesslike, professional approach is not only the right way, it's the only way. You might make some brief gains by making ultimatums, but believe me those gains will be brief. If you're viewed as a gimme guy or gal whose only interest is in weaseling as much as possible out of the company, your long-term future will be doomed. If you have your hand out (and there's nothing wrong with having your hand out), be sure your motives are clear.

#1

Do your homework and research. Make sure you know how the company is doing financially, what the company's strategic business plan is, how the company's competitors are doing, etc. If you are not sure how to find out this info, talk to one of the movers and shakers in your company. Offer to take them to coffee to get the latest news and to find out what they see coming down the pike with the company. By aligning your approach to what is currently going on in the company, your chances for success will increase significantly.

#2

Present your boss with a written, business proposal format. Not a ten-page document; a one-page proposal with headlines and a two- or three-sentence description of each request. The key is to clearly show the boss how your work has helped the company achieve its goals. By taking this approach, your boss will most likely view your request in a more positive light.

#3

Demonstrate how your getting these demands met benefits the company. At first blush, it may not be clear how you getting a raise will help the company achieve its goals. But if you have kept a record of your performance, and if you can verbalize how your work has helped the company move forward, your chances for success improve exponentially. Be very specific. List in bullet point form your contributions over the past few months. Then, add a few more bullet points on how you will help the company achieve its goals (and, of course, you know what the company's goals are since you did your homework earlier) over the next few months. Understand, though, that making a profit is the prime objective for all companies. If they don't do that, *they* won't be in business, and *you* won't have to worry about asking anybody for anything. Your primary objective is to point out how what you are asking for will benefit the company; secondary, of course, is that it will benefit you, too.

Don't confront the boss brandishing ultimatums and attitude, but don't crawl in on your hands and knees, either. Be confident. After all, you're bringing something to the dance that will benefit everyone.

What If You Don't Get What You Want?

Unfortunately, that's what sometimes happens.

#1

Let's say you don't get what you want. Despite all your careful planning, the research, the preparation, and talking to all the right people, you go back to your desk empty-handed. *Drat!* Sometimes (and you may never know why) things just don't work out the way you want them to. If that happens, don't throw a tantrum, don't decide to stonewall (as in becoming part of the problem instead of becoming part of the solution) the system, don't start thinking of ways to get even. Above all, don't decide that your boss's denial means you're not a valued employee. There are lots of reasons that you may be turned down, most of them having to do with either the timing of the proposal or the fact that it doesn't fit into the overall strategy of the company. But the only guarantee that you'll never be turned down is to never ask—a hopeless, self-defeating strategy.

#2

Revisit your request and decide what you'd be willing to change. Whenever I've been turned down (hey, it happens to the best of us), I've asked for permission to revisit the request at some future date. You want to secure the opportunity to go back through your proposal, see if there are some concessions you could make, or add something you missed the first time around. A great way to find out how you "missed the mark" with your first proposal is to ask for specific feedback from your boss, or even from respected colleagues. Your boss may say, "I like your proposal, but these items need to be addressed." Listen to what she has to say, and be sure to highlight the issues she pointed out when you present your request a second time.

#3

If your requests are continually being rejected, it may be a sign that your boss isn't receptive to new ideas, or maybe the company itself doesn't welcome that kind of input. If you're approaching the matter in a professional, confident way and regularly being told "no" (even though you feel that your proposals have merit), it may be time to consider employment at a company more open to the kind of initiative you have to offer.

Have a Coach Help You

You don't have to hire a career coach to give you pointers on how to ask for more. A good friend will do just fine. I don't recommend spouses because there may be too much emotion (and not enough clarity) involved, but it should be someone you respect and trust.

#1

The coach's role is to listen to what you have to say, clarify any questions they (or your boss) might have, discuss some potential strategies, and support your effort with loads of encouragement. Find someone you trust who will give you some good, unemotional feedback and you'll be starting off on the right foot.

#2

Decide prior to the first meeting what you hope to accomplish each meeting and what each person's role will be. In short, establish the ground rules. Then, establish a time to meet regularly. Every Tuesday at seven o'clock for fifteen minutes, or maybe every Wednesday over coffee. Pick a regularly scheduled time and stick to it. If you don't, it's easy for other things to take precedence. Try to make it a face-to-face meeting; you'll get more accomplished. If that's not possible, a phone conversation will do. But do it. However you choose to meet, be strict about sticking to your schedule.

#3

Practice role playing with your coach. Lots of people are uncomfortable meeting with the boss, and your new and creative ideas will go ignored if you don't present them, and yourself, with confidence and flair. The only way to get over your nervousness is to practice what you want to say, and perfect how you want to say it. Role playing will help. Even though I still had more than a few butterflies in my stomach the first time I went to my boss with a request, role playing had given me enough confidence to actually do it. A coach should give you feedback on everything from your voice inflections to your posture to your level of eye contact to how fast you're talking.

As I've outlined in this chapter, if you confront your boss in a professional manner, chances are good that you'll get what you're asking for. Remember that if you're a solid or a star performer, they need you as much as you need them (perhaps even more if you're a star). You now have some power, some leverage in the negotiations. Use it.

I'm going to take the liberty of using myself as a case study. (I'm the best example I know. I can't help it.) In late 1991 I was employed by Haworth, a two-billion-dollar, privately owned manufacturer of office furniture, as a senior account rep in the Denver office. I was doing well and had just won a major project, when an expanded territory became available. I knew the opportunity for a promotion, including a new title and more money, existed, and the timing was right. I did my homework by talking to a few people in our corporate division and finding out how they viewed this new territory and what they envisioned for its future development and incorporated the information into my plan. I scheduled an appointment with my boss, the Western Regional Manager, made a thirty-minute verbal presentation (I set it up so he could ask questions during this part of the presentation), followed by a written proposal confirming what I had just presented. I wanted to convince him that it made sense to cover this additional territory (Utah and Idaho) from the Denver office since the company wouldn't have to hire another person until the sales volume justified it. I pitched my idea confidently and enthusiastically, making sure that my boss understood how the new arrangement would be good for the company, and in the end he bought the idea. Six months later I proposed that since that business was now doing so well in Utah and Idaho, thanks to my efforts, I wanted to move to Salt Lake City for two years, develop the business there, then turn the territory over and move back to Denver.

Because I had a good idea, did my research, and approached my boss in a professional manner, I went from being a senior account rep to being a territory, essentially multistate manager. With that promotion came a significant raise in compensation, increased authority, a stronger presence in the company, a better bonus plan, and telecommuting privileges.

#4

At another company where I worked, I was the GM for a division and Craig was a systems engineer for that group. When a merger occurred, Craig presented to me a business proposal stating that he wanted to receive a promotion based on the fact that, as the companies merged, he would become a team leader and be responsible for integrating the two groups and getting them to work together. He didn't just waltz into my office after the merger and demand more money to compensate for his added responsibilities. He did his homework, contacting sources inside and outside the company to ask what they thought would help facilitate a timely and thorough integration of the two teams. He went to the experts and sent up the well known trial balloon. He also had the advantage of knowing my management style and having a good idea of what kind of suggestions would appeal to me.

His proposal said that if he was successful in getting his two groups to gel, that he would be given a promotion and an increase in compensation. It was a win-win deal. The good news is that he did it. His new title is Director of Systems Engineering for the combined companies. More money. More opportunities. He asked for more and he got it. Why? He did it the right way.

Chapter Nine: Exercises

For most of us, the prospect of asking for a raise is terrifying. Before we dive into strategy, let's take a moment for some confidence building. (Your critic is bound to argue with what's written below, so your job is to keep him in check. Banish him to the basement or the garden shed for a half hour.)

All of us (and I do mean all of us) sometimes feel that we're not very valuable. We think that others could do it better. We're just not good enough. Even when we're doing well, eventually people will find out the truth, that we were just lucky, not talented or particularly skilled. Your boss feels this way sometimes. So did your favorite teacher in high school. So does the next door neighbor, the guy in the next cubicle, even the person who's competing with you for a promotion in the company. What you need to know is that FEAR OF NOT BEING GOOD ENOUGH IS **UNIVERSAL!** Why? Who knows? We'll leave that question to psychologists and philosophers (although it probably has something to do with that inner critic we all have). Knowing this truth, however, gives you a huge advantage in your career. *Feeling "not good enough" simply proves you're human, not that you're inadequate or unworthy. You can feel "not good enough" and still ask for, and receive, a raise.*

How to Overcome Feeling "Not Good Enough"
You have to start telling a different story about yourself. You could probably give me plenty of evidence that you're not good enough: the time when you dropped the fly ball at a crucial moment during a Little League game. The time when you asked that pretty girl to dance and she said no. The time you got a B in math when your best friend got an A. The time when you missed a deadline at work. *Everyone* has their examples of these. They prove nothing except that you're human. They only become a problem if you interpret them to mean that you're a loser, and start to believe that to be true.

If you want a successful career, you have to begin gathering evidence for a different story: that you're good enough, and that you get stuff done (remember the GSD degree?).

EXERCISE 1

1. Think of ten things you have accomplished in your career. They don't have to be spectacular, they just have to show that you get stuff done. Build a case, based on evidence from your past, that you get stuff done. List your home runs, your extra-base hits, even your really-well-timed singles. Keep them in a file or a journal which you can refer to whenever your critic attacks and tries to make you feel like you're a loser.

2. Starting today, begin an accomplishment list. Rather than crossing items off a "to do" list as you complete them, write them onto an accomplishment list. Keep it where you can see it. When you start to feel "not good enough" (sounds like a critic attack to me), refer to your list for evidence that you get stuff done.

3. Using your imagination and elements of your career map, project yourself forward one year in time and write a fictional accomplishment list for the next twelve months. What were the things you got done? If one or two of your ideas appeal, write down the actions that preceded their accomplishment.

Truth is, you can feel "not good enough" and still get stuff done. You can feel "not good enough" and still be a star performer.

EXERCISE 2 Strategizing for a Raise

People who are successful in receiving raises and other forms of additional compensation have the following elements in place.

- Confidence in their own value and worth

- A track record of strong performance

- Good timing

- A strong and detailed proposal which benefits the company

- Awareness of the big picture for the company (you guessed it, they've done their research).

- Nonattachment to the outcome of their request (meaning that they've done their work to make "yes" more likely, but they realize that "no" is still a possible outcome, they're okay with that, and it doesn't stop them from asking for what they want).

If you have all of these in place, it might be time to make a request of your boss. Here's a suggested sequence of steps:

1. Show your proposal to at least three people who will give you honest feedback. Make revisions as necessary.

2. With timing duly considered, request a meeting with your boss.

3. Role play the meeting with your career coach/career buddy at least twice before meeting with your boss.

4. Visualize the outcome going in your favor. (Spend ten minutes twice

per day imagining the meeting going really well, your boss saying how much he likes your proposal, and shaking your hand as you agree on a deal.)

5. Be ready to suffer a critic attack. Whatever your critic says, don't let him stop you from asking for what you want. As the cliché goes, "feel the fear, and do it anyway."

6. Don't turn the meeting into a life-or-death, do-or-die scenario, a measure of whether you're a valuable human being or pond scum. It's a simple business negotiation. It might produce the intended result (a raise) or it might not.

7. Before you meet with your boss, decide which elements of your proposal are negotiable, and which are not. Have a mental list of what you're willing to give up prepared ahead of time. Then if you need to negotiate terms with your boss, you'll already have thought your strategy through.

8. When you meet with your boss, BREATHE! Be direct and clear about your request. Don't talk too much. Listen lots.

9. Have a few inquiries ready, such as: "What elements of this proposal do you like?" or "What doesn't work for you, and how would you like to see it changed?"

10. Whatever the outcome, thank your boss for his/her time, and acknowledge his continued support of your career development.

Unconventional Career Paths: The New Look of Work

M any of the ideas I offer in this book to help you build a better career, while not revolutionary, can certainly be considered unconventional. Why is thinking outside the box so crucial? Because there's no such thing as "business as usual" anymore. Convention (or the usual) started sliding out the door when the new workplace rules began to take over in the late eighties and early nineties, when companies essentially tore up the old employment contract and began to reinvent themselves. In this chapter I'm going to concentrate on some particularly unconventional approaches to career paths. Approaches that at first may seem like tactics you wouldn't be interested in doing. But keep this in mind as you read this chapter: Many of these ideas will become mainstream in the next couple years (if they haven't already). Here's your chance to get ahead of the curve in managing your career.

One of the questions that clients often ask when we talk about various new strategies is, how do companies feel about job jumping, or someone who would rather be an independent contractor than an employee; in essence, what do they think of this whole concept of being a free agent? Younger companies today are very positive about it because it fits in well with the new way of doing business. Because they have to reinvent themselves on a daily basis, they need to be very flexible and fluid to compete in the volatile environment in which most companies operate. They want people who thrive on risk and are not afraid of change. A fluid workforce can fuel companies with a lot of new ideas, hence job jumping is acceptable and not looked down upon.

The reengineering of corporate America is an opportunity, not a threat. Downsizing, outsourcing, and the like are not necessarily bad things; as a matter of fact, we can make them work to our advantage. Harry Dent, author of *The Roaring 2000s*, says that the new economy will be clearly established by the year 2007. In other words, the early nineties was a transitional phase and business is about to have a whole new look. But don't panic—you've got a few years to rethink your career. In fact, the next five or six years should be a great window of opportunity for you.

One of the benefits of an unconventional career path is that you gain a lot more personal freedom. Instead of being tied (shackled?) to the company like we were for decades, we are now free to take advantage of the exciting opportunities, or even create our own. Today we know that skills transfer—what you learn in one job can help you excel in another, even if the positions seem to have nothing in common. I don't know why it took us this long to appreciate this fact. Remember, too, that there are lots of things that matter more in life than your formal level of education. Don't forget the Get Stuff Done Degree. Once people find out you have one of those, your market value rises exponentially. What's important today are your creative thinking skills, people skills, problem solving skills, and your ability to be a change agent.

Once, we more or less built our lives around our jobs. Now we are probably more likely to build our jobs around our lives. That's part of the new, important work/life balance we're striving for. Unconventional career paths are going to give us more control over our lives, more input, and therefore more balance.

I worked in corporate America and built my life around my job. The company said go; I went. They said stay; I stayed. They said jump; I said, how high? My relationship with my wife, my kids, my neighbors, everything took place in relationship to the job. Now I get to work another way—my way.

There are two primary career paths I'm going to talk about. One is strategic job jumping, the other is becoming an independent contractor or consultant. Both are a form of free agency.

Free Agency

This is not so much an actual career path, but a state of mind. Companies have always had the right to let you go any time they felt like it; and they could always find a reason. Always. You didn't (and still don't) have a lifetime contract. The cradle to grave deal, where you went to work at the same plant your father and grandfather spent all their working years, is part of the vanishing American workplace landscape. Poof! Up in smoke. Like Samuel Gompers and the turn-of-the-century labor movement, it's all history now. ▷

Free agency then, is a state of mind, not an employment contract, not a written agreement you have with a company. If you understand that you've always been a free agent, that you've never had any real job security, then maybe you'll have an easier time moving in that direction.

Having accepted the harsh reality of the workplace, adopting a free agency state of mind doesn't mean you can cop an attitude of "Screw you, Company." I'm just trying to emphasize that the company's primary objective is to make a profit. If you fit into that scenario, great. If you don't, you might end up with a pink slip in your pay envelope. But when you're working for them, you give that company your loyalty and 110 percent effort. That's the only way to work.

There are four ways to prepare yourself for free agenthood.

#1 Know Yourself

It's amazing to me that so few people choose careers and jobs that match or reflect who they are and what they want out of life. They take a job that pays the bills, they show up on time, go through their daily routine while carefully watching the clock, and buzz out the door at 5:00 P.M. sharp. I can almost guarantee you that those people live the rest of their lives the same way. You need to know who you are (and not only in the workplace) and what will lead you to fulfill your greatest potential. What is your sense of purpose? How do you want to contribute to the world? What's the best path towards self-awareness? Mantras, meditation, going to the mountains, sitting cross-legged, it's up to you, but make an effort to find out. It may be the most important discovery of your life. And it will definitely have an impact on your work. And possibly your bowling score.

One last thing on this heavy-does-it subject: I have known people who have had a major struggle with finding balance with their work/life issues. Specifically folks who want to be of service to mankind, but also need to pay the rent and send the kids to school. There is no easy answer. But the people who seem to be happiest are the ones who came to a place where they accepted that the real world still held a lot of the cards, and that focusing on having balance was the best compromise.

#2 Identify Your Strengths and Weaknesses

Once you've tapped into who you are, how you want to live, what kind of work will most appeal to your temperament, you need to identify your strengths and your weaknesses so you can better understand where you fit in the workplace. Be very open and honest with yourself. Think of it as a self-inventory. Make a list of your weaknesses so you can take steps (classes, instruction, etc.) to remedy them. When you interview for a job, however, if you're asked what do you consider your weaknesses, be truthful.

When I decided to make the jump from office products to computers (technology), I noted in my personal inventory that I had a number of strengths that were related to my people skills and my problem-solving skills that would continue to work to my advantage no matter where, or in what industry, I was employed. On the other hand, I didn't know diddly (or at least not very much) about being a database administrator or a software programmer. The on/off switch sometimes turned out to be something of a challenge. So when I was interviewing for work, I would always tell my interviewer that if they were looking for a programmer, or a Web site manager, I wasn't the guy. But I also stressed the fact that I didn't believe those things would in any way hinder my performance. I played to my strengths as an experienced and creative problem solver with proven people skills. You know, the GSD guy.

What else can you do if asked the dreaded "what are your weaknesses" question? Here are a couple of tips:

1. Understand that there is a good chance that question will come up. By knowing that in advance, you'll have some time to get yourself ready instead of being totally surprised.

2. Come up with the two or three weaknesses you think are most applicable. Be honest here, but don't throw yourself under the bus, either.

3. Ask a good friend or fellow business buddy that you admire what they think of your choices. Do they agree? How would they answer the question if asked? The idea here is to be clear in your answer before you go to the interview.

4. Think in terms of how you have turned a weakness into a strength in the past. Give actual examples whenever possible. For example: I once had the weakness of being impatient with my fellow workers' lack of willingness to "do

what it takes" to get a project done. Instead of yelling and screaming at them (which never really works) I figured out a plan to give them extra time off if we could get the project done ahead of schedule. Guess what? They loved it (who doesn't love time off?). We finished two full days ahead of schedule.

5. Practice your answers with a friend. It will help you get comfortable and look confident during the interview.

6. If you decide you want to get more formal help on these issues, check out your local adult-education center. It's pretty common for them to have classes on interviewing, public speaking, and the like.

#3 Homework, Homework, Homework

It's incredibly important to stay up to date with what's going on in your company, in your industry, and in the market. And you have a ready-made resource—the Internet. You can sit at home in your jammies and leisurely cruise the appropriate sites that will give you vital information about your industry. Set a time limit, maybe no more than twenty minutes at one time, or, if you're anything like me, you'll be scanning medical histories or obscure historical figures or the latest homeopathic remedies. (I can't help it. I think it's one of my weaknesses.)

Here are some sites to help you along the research trail:

1. *Hoovers.com*: This site has all sorts of info on companies and industries. Some of the info is free, some you have to pay for.

2. *Vault.com*: This site will give you the lowdown on what a company is up to, including actual testimonials from current and past employees.

3. *Business2.com*: One of my favorites! It's devoted to keeping us abreast of not only what's happening in our laser-paced

business world, but is strong in predicting what's going to be happening in the next year or two.

#4 Model Yourself After Someone Who's Successfully Made the Transition

Maybe they're in the workplace, or in your family, or even the neighborhood, but find somebody who has made a successful transition from the old-school way of working to embracing their identity as a free agent. Find someone who has what you want and find out how he or she got it. (This, by the way, works in all areas of your life.) Model the behavior. Although easier said than done, this approach can be very effective. I'm not suggesting that you become a clone of someone. I'm suggesting that you pick out their traits you really admire, and begin to incorporate them in your work activities. In some cases, if the person you admire is willing to help you along this path, don't hesitate in asking them to introduce you to their network of contacts, or tell you where they buy their business outfits, or if they can recommend a great new business book to read.

Strategic Job Jumping

I read an article once where the guy referred to this strategy as "Homos Jobus Hoppus." Wish I'd have thought of it first. The beauty of this way of managing your career is that it allows us, as workers, to maintain a competitive edge and our enthusiasm.

I can't tell you how many of my clients feel that they are stuck (welded, really) to jobs which they have spent years in college preparing for, and about which they are now thoroughly disillusioned. Five years. Ten years. Bummed out. Burned out.

My job is to prove to them that their options are wide open, and one of the reasons this is true is because the new look workplace allows (and encourages) job hopping. Remember, skills are transferable. People skills, problem-solving skills, and can-do skills are what

I call "universal skills": They apply everywhere. The fact that I wasn't great at turning my computer on, or couldn't figure out how to reboot it when I managed to get it locked up, didn't prevent me from becoming a success in the technology industry.

You've been a nurse for ten years and now you want to try sales? You're an expert at keeping people calm and explaining why they need certain treatments they may not be sure they need—how is that different from explaining to a client why your product is going to boost their sales or streamline their manufacturing process? Dental hygienist to accountant? Why not? Hygienists' attention to detail is incredible. It's the same skill that is needed in accounting. Job hopping is a strategy that allows you to do that.

Another great benefit of the strategy is that it often allows you to significantly increase your earning capacity. Staying at the same job for years and years pretty much guarantees that your salary increases will be in the 4, 5, or 6 percent range. But a nurse that was a client of mine, who eventually took a job in sales, tripled her salary within the first two years. The company you jump to also benefits through your new ideas and skills that the twenty-year employee may not have needed to develop. By hiring free agents or consultants, they have the flexibility to be able to adjust their own workforce at a moment's notice, and they welcome people who are adaptable and understand the nature of the new workplace.

First of all, you should think of job jumping as a career strategy. It's not something you do because you're upset with your boss or you don't like the new office where your company has relocated. The old modus operandi was "Stay at the same job for forty years and retire." More recently, we were told "Change jobs every five to seven years." But I'm telling you, you don't need to wait even that long. When I changed jobs four times in five years it wasn't because I was easily bored, it was a career strategy. During that short period of time I tripled my pay, averaging an increase of almost 40 percent a year. It wasn't just about more money, it was also about getting new assignments and more responsibility. Interestingly enough, not one of my new employers asked me why I changed jobs so often. Part of that was because I came to the interview well prepared (mini business plan, etc.), but another part of it was because my attitude fit so well with the company philosophy.

Second, identify and target what the hot industries are, and what top companies are within the field that interests you. Here's a list of the top ten growth industries for the year 2000:

1. High-tech

2. Communications

3. Business services

4. Medical/pharmaceutical

5. Electronics

6. Financial services

7. Health care

8. Manufacturing

9. Consumer products

10. Media and entertainment

You don't want to be in an industry that's going downhill, like the carbon paper business. You don't want to join a company that's going downhill, like a newspaper type-setting firm. And the only way you're going to avoid them is to do your research.

Part of your research can include networking; it's an old, conventional technique that's stood the test of time. It still works: people talking to people. Don't be afraid to ask questions. What's available? Who's available? When? Join an industry organization (e.g., The Rocky Mountain Mass Spectrometer Users Group, affectionately known as ARMSUG), go to career fairs, talk to business leaders. You should always be networking, talking about what's going on in the market, staying current with industry trends, introducing yourself to people "in the know."

Now that you've targeted the industry you're interested in and the company you want to work for, use your favorite search engine to cruise the Internet for specific information about them. Read all the available publications. Your local library and/or favorite bookstore can help you identify the best sources, or query people you respect in the business community about how they keep up to speed on the latest happenings in their industry.

Steer clear of the conventional, answer-the-want-ad, send-the-résumé technique. You'll go farther and make a better impression if you do your research, identify an industry, target a company, and present a mini business plan that describes what you'll be able to bring to the dance.

Market yourself to the targeted industry (just a brief mention here because I'm going to cover it at length in the next chapter). In today's dynamic, fast-moving, ever-changing workplace, you cannot sit back and wait for the mountain to move your way. Take your bones to the mountain, brother (and sister), pack the right equipment (shoes, mini business plan, backpack, research, granola) and start your ascent.

The next step is winning the great job. You've written your job proposal and your mini business plan, done your research, topped it off with a great interview by stressing what you're going to be able to do for the company (thereby differentiating yourself from the competition, who are trying to find out what the company's going to do for *them*), and so . . . the job is yours.

The next step in strategic job jumping is to have an immediate, positive impact on the job. At one time there was plenty of time to make your mark. There were yearlong training programs, sometimes lasting even two years, and you weren't expected to be productive right off the bat. But not today. What companies want is someone who is an immediate player, someone who brings value to the table from day one. You've got your plan; go ahead and put it into action. Your initiative and productivity increases your own value, too, so that when you get ready to make your next move to job jump, you leave with a track record that sparkles with accomplishments. The prospective employer can see how quickly you came up to speed and made an impact at (what will soon become) your old company.

Since you're using job jumping as a career strategy, moving

every one to three years, you don't have time to loiter at the fringes and drift slowly into the organization. You need to be an impact player from the start, though *not* at the expense of trashing relationships or not helping others to achieve their own goals. Remember: *A high tide raises all boats.* It is not necessary to climb the ladder using discarded bodies as rungs. You can get ahead without being ruthless.

Whenever possible, involve your team members in all important decisions; like how to improve certain workflow processes, or how to get a project done on schedule, or what hours the store should stay open. You will probably enjoy how teammates will respond when asked to participate in decision-making discussions. There is no need to take credit for everything your team produces, either. Managers have a way of knowing who's doing the bulk of the work, who's driving the project and who's along for the ride. Carving out a special kingdom for yourself will eventually lead to a very lonely existence. At one time, building an empire of your own was a strategy that worked. If you hoarded all the marbles, you could dictate who could play. But today companies want team players, people who know how to work well with others and get things done.

If you see a problem developing, quickly present a proposal to management detailing how you would solve it. They may not accept or act on your proposal (they may not even acknowledge the problem), but I guarantee you they'll be impressed with your approach. Today's bosses don't just want to hear "I think we've got a problem." While they're interested in the potential dilemma, they're even more interested in a possible solution. I used to tell the people that worked for me not to come to me with a problem unless they had thought of at least one way to solve it. In writing, if you please. As a proposal.

The last step in the job-jumping strategy is to start looking for your next position. In fact, I advocate that you *always* be looking for your next deal. Maybe not actively sending out résumés and scouting parties, but always researching, always networking, always looking for the next opportunity. And it's absolutely imperative that you leave your current job when you're on top. Leave at the crest of the wave, not the trough. Leave when you're the star, when you've just won the award as the Employee of the Year, and finished the year at 150 percent of quota.

If you're a ballplayer, you don't test the free agent market after you've hit .230 and had a terrible year in the field. The philosophy works the same way in business. Leave just after they have a ticker tape parade in your honor. You'll be in such demand that you'll have your pick of companies wanting you to come score for their team.

Remember that this is a career strategy. It's a way to stay current, to have more freedom, to meet new challenges, and to have more fun (don't *ever* forget the fun factor). It's how you're going to move quickly into the better jobs with the bigger compensation packages.

Become an Independent Contractor/Consultant

Everyone is a business, including you. An independent contractor can either work full-time at the customer's site, or be a home-based, or small office-based business. In recent years the latter way of contracting has become extremely popular. Telecommuting isn't just something we wistfully dream about; it's a vibrant reality in today's market. There are some business analysts who forecast that, in a few years, a third of the workforce will be telecommuting. The company reduces their infrastructure cost by having less office space, less office furniture, etc. Employees like it because they're not fighting traffic every day, they have more freedom and better life/work balance; plus, according to a recent survey by the American Management Association, telecommuters get more done because of less office politics and fewer interruptions and distractions.

Here's how you can be most effective as an independent contractor/consultant.

#1

If you're working out of a home office, don't stay there all day; take some time and get out into the marketplace. Meet with clients, with vendors, with fellow workers. Why? Because some of us have a tendency to forget that there is more to our work than writing reports. We need to continue to add new relationships that can help us down the road, or reinforce the relationships we already have.

#2

Don't spend too much time on your personal computer at home. People tend to get lost in some wonderful backwater (that has nothing to do with their business) and spend hours and hours watching the alligators. It's wasted time; you'll end up spending twelve hours getting eight hours' worth of work done.

#3

Focus on servicing your customer better, rather than on growing your business. There's a tendency when you first leave the sheltering warmth of corporate America to start on your own, to focus on building your business and getting more customers. Without the comfort of a steady paycheck, we tend to panic and sometimes forget our existing customers. The proper focus should be on giving your current customers unparalleled service; better than anyone else could provide.

#4

Don't think in terms of a formal, rigid, multiyear, traditional business plan to guide you down the road of success. When you're an independent contractor, you've got to be extremely flexible, able to respond to exactly what the market's doing. For example, if you're a contracted salesperson for a computer dealer, and the manufacturers are bypassing the dealers by selling their products directly to the corporate end-users, you might want to focus your efforts on selling computer-related services instead of just products. And even though you have chosen a specific course, always maintain the adaptability to allow you to change direction should the need arise. It's not uncommon that companies sell off divisions, or change basic business strategies with no notice, putting consultants out of an engagement. If you have kept yourself multidimensional in your skills, the chances of you being dumped are less.

#5

Don't let business run your life. Once you're clear of the corporate claws and on your own, it's easy to feel overwhelmed. Just stay focused and remember that you'll be happiest if you achieve a work/life balance—balance being the key word. By balance, I mean the ability to take your kids to a school event in the middle of the afternoon, or go catch an afternoon baseball game when your favorite team is in town. You may have to work late that night to get an assignment done, but at least you had a choice in the matter.

One of the things I suggest to clients who are drawn to being an independent contractor is that they propose the idea to their employer. Show them a mini business plan that lists what you'll be able to accomplish beyond what you can do now. "Here's what I'll be able to do for you . . ." You'll probably be surprised at how many companies will be open to giving your proposal a go.

I've also seen groups of people, whole departments, the accounting department or the advertising department, approach management with a proposal similar to the one an individual would use. That is, you spell out the advantages to the company of why it makes sense for them to outsource the department to the newly formed company of their ex-employees. One such example was Entex, who contracted their public relations needs to the folks who had been the company's employees in that particular department. If you make your case in clear, concise terms, indicating where the company can save money on the bottom line, you'll at least get a careful hearing. Guaranteed.

Here are, in my opinion, the best fields in which to become a home-based or independent contractor/consultant.

1. Accounting

2. Advertising/PR

3. Career coaching

4. Editing/writing

5. Janitorial

6. Market research

7. Telemarketing

8. Office productivity (word processing, secretarial, etc.)

9. Tax planning

10. Technology (Web site developers, network engineers, etc.)

Becoming an independent contractor is clearly the hottest trend in the workplace right now. You get to make decisions about what is essentially your own business. But to be successful you've got to make a bigger commitment in terms of being willing to do whatever it takes to get the job done, maybe than you ever have (which doesn't mean working longer hours). Just keep in mind that the benefits are enormous—more freedom, more control of your working time, better work/life balance, to name just a few.

The downsides are few, but they do exist. The first is that you may not get a paycheck every two weeks (although independent contractors make an average of 40 percent more than salaried workers). If that makes you nervous, factor it into your decision. Second, you won't have the benefit package you once had. More and more insurance companies, however, are willing to offer great group rates to the independents. You may pay a little more, but it won't be much. Third, you won't have that office camaraderie. But just think, you also won't have to deal with that jerk who tells the awful jokes.

And if you're going to *be* a business, you're going to have to *act* like a business. Companies will look at you a little differently than they did when you were an employee. You're now a business owner. Act the part. Be your own greatest fan. Believe in what you're doing. Confidence is contagious.

Case Studies

Two years ago Mark came to me as a highly skilled and highly successful technical project manager in the computer services business. He loved his job, but if he was assigned to a project for any considerable length of time, he got bored and lost interest. And working for the big computer services companies, he might get stuck on a job for a year or more. He admitted that he was happier and more satisfied when he worked on shorter projects. Mark was a prime candidate for becoming an independent contractor.

We worked together on a game plan and decided that he would do best by marketing himself as an expert in a particular area of project management, in this case desktop migration projects. As an independent contractor, he went to all the big companies in the Denver area and marketed himself with that expertise. How did he market himself? He simply developed a list of fifty target companies whom he thought might need his services. He then sent a one-page description of his new consulting firm to the CIO (Chief Information Officer) of each firm. This inexpensive piece listed his areas of expertise, the certifications he had received, and a list of similar projects he had successfully completed. Within weeks he had secured several projects. Today, he has a thriving business working only the projects he wants, works out of his home, has lots of freedom and the work/life balance he had always dreamed of.

The second example is yours truly. Though I worked in corporate America for twenty-five years with some degree of success, it finally became clear to me (I never said I was a quick study) that I worked best outside the normal restrictions imposed on anyone laboring within the system. Through a process of self-assessment, identifying my strengths and my weaknesses, I decided that I needed and wanted a job with far more freedom.

Although I had adapted a job-jumping career strategy years prior, three years ago I decided I was ready for another change. I took my own advice and consulted with several people I knew and respected to get some feedback about my strengths and weaknesses. The feedback I got about my strengths was that I had hired and trained hundreds of people over the years. I was, in fact, a good career coach. So I decided to make career coaching a full-time profession. It would allow me to work out of my home and have the personal freedom to be creative without being hindered by a lot of policies and procedures. I knew there would be risk involved in becoming an independent contractor, but it seemed more worthwhile than the risk involved in staying with the company.

Although it wasn't part of my original vision to build a national company, I have now grown the business from a one-person shop to over three hundred coaches across the United States. We are now expanding the business into the fifty biggest cities and have built a state-of-the-art Web site to support the coaches and our clients. And guess what? Even though I loved working out of my home for a period of time, I have still been able to maintain some of the freedom and ability to do the work I want even in the new company.

Think about what it is you want to do. Create a strategy. Then do it.

Chapter Ten: Exercises

There's more than one way to skin a cat (although I'm not advocating that as a high-reward career direction in a growth industry). No two people are alike, and their career paths should be equally divergent. The key is to know what you want, what kind of career path would bring out the best in you, and what you need to stay productive and satisfied in the long term. These exercises are designed to help you evaluate whether a nontraditional career path will fit your personality.

EXERCISE 1 Should You Job Jump?

Here's a formula for deciding if job-jumping fits your career: answer the following questions according to the following scale:

1. Strongly agree.   **2. Sometimes true, sometimes not.**   **3. Doesn't really sound like me.**

_____ I love change. Variety is one of the main fuels of my career.

_____ I am most productive when I have regular changes in my environment.

_____ I am most productive when I have regular changes in responsibility.

_____ I am currently successful in my job, and confident about my value to my current employer.

_____ I do not need to change jobs for any urgent reason (financial crisis, change of location, avoiding the repo man, just got the boss's daughter pregnant).

_____ I enjoy marketing and branding myself, networking, and following through on leads.

_____ I am positioned (i.e., skilled, trained) to work in an industry that has high turnover, or is undergoing significant expansion or change in market behavior.

_____ I can make a difference for an employer in a short length of time. I don't take a year to learn to be effective in a new job.

_____ My career path is not primarily motivated by a desire for security and predictability.

_____ I have a career map, and changing jobs several times in the next few months will enhance my prospects of reaching my stated career goals.

_____ TOTAL POINTS

Evaluation:

26–30: You're ready to begin job jumping. You have created a foundation from which job jumping can be a successful and profitable career strategy.

18–25: Job jumping is a *potentially* good strategy for you, but you're not quite ready yet. If you like the idea, begin to position yourself to become a hot commodity. Go back to chapters 5 and 6 on being a change agent and star performer, make positive steps in those directions, and retake this test.

0–17: Find a more traditional career path. There are still some out there, and they represent a viable career strategy. Look for a company in a stable industry that values loyalty, retains workers by offering them a package of benefits that emphasize security.

EXERCISE 2 Should You Become a Free Agent?

Take a look back at your career map. What do you want your career to produce? If your answer is something like "freedom, independence, and variety" (sounds like a campaign slogan), free agency may be for you. If your answers read more like "security, community, and consistency" this may not be the way to go.

Research:

- Find at least three people who have successful free-agent careers. Interview them, and find out what they most like and dislike about being a free agent.

Action:

- Write down your known core competencies. This is what you will be selling as a free agent, and will be the foundation of your success. How could you leverage them into a successful free-agent business? Begin to construct a business plan on this foundation.

- Now (you knew this was coming) write down your weaknesses. Begin to consider how these might sabotage you, and what you can do to prevent this from occurring. With whom could you team to fill in the gaps in your competency?

More research:

- Go back to your free agent friends. Show them your preliminary business plan. Get specific feedback. Ask them what they would do if they were in your position.

- Find an inside coach in the industry you've targeted, and ask them how you might leverage your core competencies to be of maximum value in that industry.

EXERCISE 3 The Introvert/Extrovert Paradox

There's a paradox about free agency. To be successful in any free agent field, you have to be able to market yourself, network successfully, find and land the work. Extroverts typically enjoy this aspect of the free agent career path. But being a free agent means being in business for yourself, which often leads to working alone much of the time. This appeals to introverts, and often repels extroverts. Which leads to this piece of advice:

The Extrovert:

If you're an extreme extrovert who needs company, companionship, and camaraderie in order to love your career, **don't create a business where you work alone.** No matter how much money you make, you'll hate the isolation. Look for partnerships, cooperatives and other group free-agent endeavors.

The Introvert:

If you're an extreme introvert, **don't design a business that requires constant marketing, networking, and public visibility.** You'll avoid it, procrastinate, fail to sell your service effectively, and go broke as a result. Either hire an extrovert (i.e., sales/marketing person) who can generate the work for you, or find a business where you have a contract which guarantees you enough work.

Bottom line? Free agency is like every other career path. That is, not for everyone. It has to fit your personality and career aspirations to be successful. Entrepreneurship may be worshipped as an American idyll, but so's being slim, athletic, and young. Your personality is what it is, just like your body type. Wishing it were different ("I'd like to be a muscular 6'2" please.") doesn't make it so. To be successful, align your career with who you are and what you want, and give up forever the idea of becoming something you're not in order to be successful in your career. Like marrying someone with the intent of changing them, IT DOESN'T WORK!

To evaluate whether you are an introvert or extrovert, we recommend taking a Myers-Briggs test. The introvert/extrovert distinction is one of the primary elements of that personality typing system. Most good books on the Myers-Briggs system will explain what introverts and extroverts need in order to succeed. However, to get the most out of this test, we recommend you work with a career coach who is familiar with this technology, and can help you to understand how it applies to you and your career choices.

The Marketing of Brand You

Here's a strange question: How do we get companies or prospective employers to chase *us?* Novel idea, huh? Well, believe it or not, the traditional pyramid of power is becoming inverted and the worker is turning out to be king. Long live the king!!

In the early seventies, if you wanted to have a great job, or work for a great company, you had to pursue them with a single-minded intensity that would have put Attila the Hun to shame. But because of a robust economy and a tight labor market, companies are actively chasing us.

Why? The simple supply-and-demand dynamic that we talked about earlier. There aren't enough great workers to go around. At long last, great driven, committed, talented people like you are in the driver's seat. About time, I'd say.

But don't be misled into thinking that just because the balance of power has shifted, you're automatically going to get that terrific job or that big raise or that promotion or stock option. Even though there's a shortage of workers out there, there's still a highly competitive environment for the top positions. One of the reasons for this is that employees are changing jobs a lot more often than they did, moving from company to company—job jumping—in search of new and better opportunities.

The way to put yourself in the best possible light, no matter what your situation at your current job, is to market yourself as brand **You.**

Tom Peters, the workplace futurist and author of *In Search of Excellence,* says that companies are finally beginning to realize that their soft assets—people and intellectual properties—are their most valuable assets.

But if you note the star performers, the people who get the big raises, the advancements, and the stock options, they are people who have established an identity for themselves within the company. Think about what brand names have done for companies over the years; there aren't too many of us who aren't aware of the Nike name, the logo or the "Just Do It" slogan that goes with it. Think McDonald's and Tommy Hilfiger. Remember what Sears meant to a whole generation (or two) in the postwar years. You got it from Sears because it was reliable and if it broke, they'd come fix it. Value. Trust. Brand name recognition. The brand is a promise of value to be received.

The same is true for people. Companies look at their employees in the same light. What picture do I get when I think of brand Frank? Reliable, energetic, hardworking. Helen? Resourceful, a can-do person, takes the initiative.

In today's marketplace, you need to think of yourself as brand **You,** as the CEO of Me, Incorporated. Everybody can do it; it's not limited to the so-called elite or the extroverts. You can establish brand **You** in your own way (tips to follow). I know the idea of marketing yourself like a product is a little scary, and certainly a little foreign, but it's absolutely critical in today's workplace.

Brand You Self-Analysis

Here are ways to check how strong your brand presently is.

#1

Make a list of the three or four things that you currently think you're known for in the workplace. Be honest with yourself. For example, you might be the top salesperson, or you might be known for being friendly and helpful. Get it? Okay. Then list two or three things that, in one year, you will add to the list.

#2

Identify three or four ways that your current work or project is provocative and challenging. For me the fact that each of my clients is unique is both challenging and provocative. If you're up to your elbows in corporate America, you may find the fact that you're often handcuffed by the bureaucracy to be your biggest challenge. (Understand that some people are motivated by negative challenges, others by positive challenges. Your job is to figure out which kind works for you and then follow that path going forward.)

#3

List at least three new things you've learned in relationship to work (in the last three or four months) that will help advance your career.

#4

What are the two or three things (a more prestigious title, performance awards, a column in the company newspaper) that would
give you more of a marketing presence (regional or national) than
those you're using on your present job? For example, I was with Entex in 1995 when we won an eighty-million-dollar contract that got
a lot of national exposure. That's certainly a marketing presence.

#5

List names of five important contacts that you've added to your
Rolodex or to your address book on your computer in the last ninety
days.

#6

List two important relationships that you've worked on improving
in the last ninety days.

#7

What's the one thing you think you need to work on in the next
ninety days to make your résumé look better?

So there you have it—seven easy steps to do a self-analysis of
the current brand **You.** How do you perceive yourself? How are you
perceived by others? What are you doing to help improve the situation?

Now that you have a somewhat better idea of where you're currently positioned in the workplace, I'm going to teach you a four-
step process to improve that position. It happens to be my personal
belief that career satisfaction starts with taking responsibility for
your own fortune. There may have been a time when the company
was more in charge of your destiny, but that's hardly the case anymore. There was also a time when years-on-the-job had some rela-

tionship to job security, but as we've already established, that's gone, too. Companies today want people with problem solving skills, creative skills, with the ability to integrate technology with people, and interpret what customers need.

The Marketing of Brand You in Four Steps

1. Define Your Product

Your goal is to create a desirable package for your product (which is, of course, brand **You**). You have to determine why you're unique, why Company ABC should 1) hire you, 2) move you forward in the company, or 3) give you stock options, bonuses, etc. What's different and special about you that will separate you (in a positive manner) from the other three hundred candidates that just marched through the office? Your own trademark, so to speak.

Starbucks is a good example of that kind of marketing. Coffee's been around for centuries. Definitely not new. So what makes Starbucks so unique? It made its mark, it defined itself as quality, as high-end coffee. The Best. It wasn't Danny's Diner with the four-bit coffee (anybody old enough to remember when coffee was a dime?). The interiors were well appointed, the lighting soft, music great, *The Wall Street Journal* in plain view. You knew this was a classy place. They raised the bar for places that sell coffee. And they charged accordingly; two or three times what you would pay anywhere else. Maybe four times if you usually eat at Danny's.

They made their mark, defined their brand as "The Best Coffee in Town." And sold it. True, the coffee's better, but the marketing was even better. They had the right product at the right time, and they were wildly successful in marketing it. You just have to say Starbucks and everyone knows you're talking about quality coffee.

The marketing of brand **You** is not so very different. Whether you're one of a hundred engineers in a software firm, or one of five receptionists, you've got to distinguish yourself in some way. Some years ago there was a receptionist at a large electronics firm who answered the phone in such a distinctive way that everybody knew who she was. People talked about her. Cathy at Hewlett-Packard. It was amazing the number of people that knew who she was because she had created a brand **Cathy** that was different. Sure, she was efficient, courteous, professional, but dozens of receptionists are and nobody remembers them. But we all remembered Cathy.

Also, is your product (you) appropriately priced? Almost everyone I know thinks they should be making more money, but either what they're bringing to the table doesn't justify it, or they haven't done a good job marketing their skills and letting the company know what they're accomplishing. So how do you know what you are worth? Once again the Internet is our friend. There are several career-related sites that tell you how much you are worth in your profession in your market. Try *erieri.com, careerpath.com,* and *rileyguide.com,* to name a few. By asking for what you are worth, you establish a value for brand **You** going forward.

Perhaps defining your product means that you need more education. Are you willing to go back to school? Are you willing to give up your nose ring to get into sales (yes, I know about personal freedom and the fact that it shouldn't make any difference if you're wearing a nose ring or not . . . but it does). To get ahead, you may have to repackage your product, get more schooling, give up some of the body armor, or turn in the Birkenstocks and start wearing socks again. It's part of the deal.

Part of how you define your product is how you identify yourself. If someone asks you what you do for a living, what do you say? If you're the quality control manager in a cheese factory, you might want to say that you're a quality control specialist with advanced analytical skills in microbiology. An accountant just as easily becomes a tax consultant (which is probably a large part of your business anyway). Same thing, different package. And as you begin to see yourself differently, other people will soon begin to view you in a different way. Understand there is a fine line here between selling your brand and turning people off. Use your own instincts to decide how far you can go with the person(s) you are speaking to at the time.

2. Determine Your Market

Who are your target customers now? Who will they be in the future? And why would they want to buy your product?

So many of my clients don't know who the important people are in their own organization. Who are the real decision makers? Who are the people who should know about what you have to offer? Having the security guard at the gate as your number-one fan because you have a winning smile is not the same thing as defining your product to someone in top management. Don't stop smiling at the guard; that's important, too. Just be sure management gets a look at your smile from time to time.

Without a clear understanding of who your audience is, you can't package yourself or create an effective marketing plan. Spend some time finding out who the movers and shakers are in your company. Dig a little if you have to. Talk to people. You might find that the people you really need to impress aren't necessarily those who are on top of the hierarchy.

3. Make a Plan

Now that you know what your product is, how you're unique, and who your market is, you're ready to make a plan. Don't write something that rivals *War and Peace;* I'm talking about a one- or two-page document that will define how you're going to move forward. You learned some valuable things in the first two steps. How are you going to utilize them? In essence you want to create your own marketing plan.

Don't go to all the trouble of making out a plan if you're not going to implement it. My clients who are most successful in moving their careers along are the ones who are willing to not only make a plan, but do the legwork and follow through. If your plan just stays on the paper and looks eloquent and dramatic believe me it won't do you a bit of good. Eloquence and a dramatic flair alone will you get somewhere only if your name is Shakespeare. William Shakespeare. The rest of us have to roll up our sleeves and get a little greasy.

I encourage my clients to go to the decision makers and the movers and discuss with them their career goals. Obvious fact: They won't know if you don't tell them. Mind readers are in short supply throughout the industry. (If you actually happen to *be* a mind reader, call me right away. I've got a great job for you.) Ask for their insight about how you would best achieve your goals. This is a very effective marketing strategy—getting input from the people who may in fact be reviewing your business plan shortly.

Part of your plan has to be to establish yourself as a solid performer. Without that, your options soon narrow to none.

Make sure the people in your company know about the positive things you've done. You don't have to get on an ego trip. When I was with Haworth, I was the number-two salesman in 1992 in the Western United States. I didn't run around telling everyone how wonderful I was and what a great salesman I was, et cetera et cetera. . . . I got the information out (important that you do), but I did it in what I hope was a diplomatic, positive way. I sent thank you notes to all the people who were significant in helping that happen: people in the finance department, people in contracts, customer service, in credit, and manufacturing. The truth is, they really *did* help me achieve my status and I wanted to thank them. It's an example of internal marketing. If you make people feel good about the job they're doing, they're going to want to help next time they get the opportunity. It's a little like the star running back taking the offensive line out for steaks from time to time. He knows he can't do it without them, and now that they know he knows, they're going to try even harder. Simple internal marketing.

Many companies have committees that they need volunteers for, a newsletter, a particular project that they need help with. Becoming involved in these "extracurricular" activities will give you some visibility and should become part of your plan.

If you've come up with a new process, a new procedure, like a better way to collect account receivables, write up a one-page mini business plan and present it to the powers that be. They'll remember you in a positive way. You'll be pegged as someone who is creative, a problem solver, someone who can get stuff done.

4. Use Effective Marketing Channels

To gain some visibility outside your present company, one of the best ways is to join and become involved in a professional or community organization. As you become an active contributor, you're going to make lots of contacts and stay abreast of trends that affect your future within your industry.

Become a relentless networker. Your best career insurance is to know lots of people, from industry contacts and acquaintances, to civic groups, church groups, even people at the gym. Don't overlook anyone. I love to tell the story about a client of mine who targeted a company he wanted to work for and asked his neighbor if he knew anybody that worked there. Turns out the neighbor worked for that particular company and ended up being a great inside coach and helping him get a job. Moral? You never know from whence help will come. But you have to ask for it.

Another good marketing channel is recruiters. If you don't know any, you will find them on the Internet, hiding in the library, even in your local phone book. Give one or two a call and explain in as much detail as possible what you want. Very simple. When the job market is tight (as it is now and will be for some time), recruiters love people like you. In prosperous times like these they don't have that many unemployed people bouncing around, so they will be very eager to be of assistance. Take them to lunch, help them by providing names of people you know who might be suitable for positions they're trying to fill. In return, the recruiter will turn to you when he finds a great job that suits your profile.

Posting your résumé on an Internet site can also be helpful. Check out the sites that are tailored to your specific agenda. You can find the site best for you by going to the "search" button and typing in your area of career interest. For example, if you are a technology professional, there's a *dice.com* and *techies.com*. If you are an executive, try *6figurejobs.com* and *headhunter.net*. Good general sites include *monster.com*, *hotjobs.com*, and *careermag.com*. Don't worry, you'll find one that meets your liking. There are over five thousand such sites to choose from.

Take advantage of the current trend in the workplace to bring people from different departments together to work on a specific project. (More on this in Chapter 12.) Volunteer for those projects, get your name out there as a doer, someone who can be counted on to help get stuff done.

Whenever possible, volunteer for assignments that will expand your skill inventory. The more you know how to do, the more valuable you are to the company. The buzzword (buzz-phrase, really) for that is "cross-functional training."

I had a client who had been a purchasing agent for years. Over time he had become typecast—Fred, the Purchasing Agent. He went to the power brokers and asked them to consider him for a couple of assignments (that had nothing to do with purchasing) that were just appearing on the horizon. Because of Fred's initiative and talents he had outside of purchasing, the company gave him the opportunity to manage a technology-based project. Fred knew, like you, that skills are transferable. Hard work, leadership, attention to detail, and thoroughness are universal skills. They are valuable and applicable whether you're an accountant or the manager of a technology project. Bottom line: The company got both a great project manager and a very happy employee.

You've got to be honest with yourself about how you need to broaden your skill set. If you find yourself tongue-tied in meetings and uncomfortable making small talk, volunteer for projects that require close interaction with others. Lots of it. And always try to work with the best people in the company; those are the people you want to get to know, the people who have the most to teach you.

Other skills that often need brushing up:

1. Creative-thinking skills: Many of us need to learn to "think outside of the box." In fact, there's a great book by that title by Mike Vance that can help you.

2. Problem-solving skills: Most companies today expect all of their employees to come to the table with answers, or at least ideas, of how to solve problems the company may be experiencing. One way for each of us to improve on that skill is to spend some time with the people you know, inside or outside your company, that seem to have a knack for problem solving. Spend some time with them (take them to lunch). Pick their brain to get a sense of the process they go through to come up with solutions. It might help you to begin to think about problems in a different light and make you more valuable to your employer.

3. Flexibility skills: This is a big one for many, many companies. Some of us are still hanging on to the old "that's not my job" operating philosophy. Get over it! Companies today need people who are able to switch thoughts and actions on a dime. Again, model yourself after the people you know who already have the talent.

Be sure every move you make meshes with your overall plan on how to market brand **You.** You need to be learning more about your business, trying to gain visibility, and improving your credentials. You're the CEO of your own company now and, as such, you're ultimately responsible for how the company **(You)** does.

One final thought. Don't forget to have fun. It is, in my humble, smalltown Iowa opinion, paramount to career success!

Chapter Eleven: Exercises

How Do You Go About Establishing Your Brand?

1. **What identity for "brand You" will most support your career objectives?** Would you benefit most by being perceived as someone who's pleasant and personable? Someone who has a GSD degree? Someone who's bright and creative?

   - Write down your own ideas about your ideal brand identity.

   - Spell out, in detail, the kinds of actions which would be consistent with this identity.

C o a c h ' s   C h a l l e n g e :

For the next month, commit to three actions per day which align with your chosen brand identity. They don't have to be grand productions, but they do have to be totally consistent with your goal. Write them down in a journal. Every last one.

---

2. **How are you currently perceived?** Interview three people who know you at work. From this information, look at what existing perceptions you must change to reach your goal.

   - Write down three actions you could take this week which would begin to change these perceptions.

3. **In unguarded moments, how do you really think of yourself?** Do you still think of yourself as the kid who was no good at math in the seventh grade? Or the one who got picked second to last for the soccer team? This is your self-image, which is roughly the same thing as your brand.

COACH'S HINT: *If you can successfully align your private self-image with your career-enhancing brand identity, other people's perceptions will automatically follow suit. This takes time. The more you act in a way that is consistent with your brand/self-image, the more evidence you build for its veracity. When you believe it, others will too. If you don't believe it, nor will anyone else. This is one of the areas where working with a career coach can make the most difference. If you discover that, despite your best efforts, you don't buy yourself as an "ideas guy" or "GSD guy," it'd be a great time to hire a coach.*

4. **Identify your "target market."** Begin to identify the individuals who must be aware of your brand. Typically, they're in decision-maker positions, but

not necessarily. Sometimes you'll target a rising star. Change these people's perception of you, and you'll have succeeded in branding yourself within your current company.

- Write down the names of ten people who are potentially part of your target market.

COACH'S HINT: *Only when you're absolutely clear on how you want to brand your-self should you communicate with these people! The keys to this are consistency and simplicity. Give people a hook to remember you by, a two- or three-word label that matches your brand identity. For example "ideas guy," "overachiever," "truth speaker," "marketing whiz."* Remember: Don't brag, distinguish.

EXERCISE 2 Branding Yourself II

If the key to branding is consistency and simplicity, your brand identity should be de-scribed accurately in one sentence, preferably just a "tag line." It's hard to get this concise on your own, and make sure that your positioning works. Here's a fun way to refine your positioning, and test it on others.

EXERCISE 3 Host a Career Party

Invite a few friends and colleagues who are motivated to achieve a successful and fulfilling career. Take turns describing your positioning, and testing your descriptor sentence or tag line on your buddies. Others can tell immediately whether it's au-thentically you, or a bit of a stretch. The goal is to produce a position which is au-thentic, simple, and alive. (By "alive," we mean something you can really get behind, get passionate about. It has to spark something in you in order to spark something in your audience.)

A successful Career Party achieves two goals. One, you get your positioning right. Two, you automatically have several people who will now think of you in this way. You've started defining your brand!

Have fun with the career party concept, and use a little imagination. I have a client who brought a bunch of old business magazines, scissors, colored paper, and glue, and had each of her friends create a career collage, a visual version of their ca-reer map. She told me that it kept her career vision alive for her far more than a dry written plan.

COACH'S HINT: *If you really want the party to be productive, you might split the cost of hiring a career coach who knows about branding yourself to moderate your get-together. Better still, pay for it yourself: Your buddies won't forget the difference you made for them.*

A Hodgepodge of Career Advice

Back in the late sixties when I was going to college there was a new show on TV called *Jeopardy!*, hosted at that time by a man named Art Fleming. Almost immediately I was hooked on the show, and since it aired in the morning, I often skipped class to watch (not that it took a whole lot for me to skip class—inclement weather of any kind was often a worthy excuse). One of my favorite categories (other than sports, which was the only thing I knew much about) was hodgepodge, a mixture of somewhat related topics. Hence the title of this chapter.

Each of the topics I'm going to address, while not deserving of its own chapter, is nonetheless an important part of the career mosaic we've been studying. Here they are, in no particular order of importance.

Project Work

In the past, most of our work was task oriented. We entered a workplace where we were given a series of tasks and responsibilities that we fulfilled on a daily basis. Some of our assignments were different (as in different customers), but essentially the task was the same every day. We either fried burgers every day, or typed letters every day, or filed lawsuits every day, but essentially, the same array of tasks every day.

What's happening today in the new workplace, is that companies are moving toward a project oriented structure. The essence of project work is that many companies now have ad hoc teams that work together for perhaps a few days or a few weeks, in some cases even longer. The goal is to solve a particular problem, address a marketing issue, create a needed service or new product. Then everyone is off to a new team, a new set of issues, a new project. I've already explained the importance of being a change agent. Business is dynamic, changing on a daily basis, consequently workers must learn to re-create their own careers and change along with it (have I repeated that enough?).

You need to get used to a more flexible, project-oriented structure where your creativity and problem solving skills will come into play.

Here are a couple of tips that may help.

If you've never been involved with project work (and many of us haven't), you'll benefit by getting some experience and practice. The way to do this is to volunteer for any project that comes along. Any project. Even though it may not seem particularly career enhancing, it's going to give you experience, and that's what you're after. You're getting some stick time, some playing time, and while you may not be playing for the big prize, you're getting the experience that you'll need later on.

The second reason to volunteer for projects is to start building your reputation within the company as a project player. You're adaptable, you get along well with team members (more on that later), you have creative ideas. All good press. And once you've been in a few projects, you can begin to be more selective about which ones you volunteer for. Next thing you know, managers wanting someone they can trust will be asking you to join them on the better projects.

Never let a project get stale. There are times in the life of a project where it can seem to be dragging on. Do your part to help the team keep moving forward by a) having daily conference calls to get updates, b) by sending out daily e-mails confirming timelines, and c) by calling fellow project teammates to ask them their feedback on an idea you have about the project. Push yourself and your teammates to make this a project you'll be proud of, that you'll be able to look back on in five years and be able to brag about.

Keep in mind that the main goal is not so much to do a good job on the project as to create surprising new ways of solving problems, or creating exciting new products and services. And, of course, to give yourself the experience you need to be a top-notch change agent.

Great Relationships

There are few things that are more satisfying in life or more important in bringing your career to the next level than the relationships you form along the way. They are critically important. You're going to have to be a little selfish—you only have so much time to give to relationships, so you'd better cultivate those that will help your career. No, this doesn't mean you should brownnose with some slug because he or she may be able to further your career. Don't even bother; it's demeaning and besides, most people can spot insincerity a mile away. Do try forming meaningful relationships— real friends—as you go up the ladder. It's just as easy and will pay off a lot more.

Think of relationships as a conduit to bring out the best in you. For example, I play tennis every Saturday with a friend I have known for years. We always have a great time, but my tennis game's not getting any better because we're both at the uniformly mediocre level. If I want my game to improve, I'm going to have to find a better tennis partner. This doesn't mean that I'm going to discard my old friend, but I'm not going to get anywhere if I don't start spending time with better players.

The first step in establishing a solid career network is to identify the kind of relationships you have now. Is there one that takes too much effort, one of those Dracula things where you can feel your energy leaking out every time you spend time with that person? Or is it a positive experience where you feel an exchange of energy? Does this person bring out the best in you? List your work relationships and rate them according to how beneficial you think they are.

Refocus all your relationships to the higher level, meaning, dump the energy draining ones and add the energy enhancing ones. And, don't, under any circumstances, befriend any more Draculas.

Understand that you only have time for so many work relationships. If you spread yourself too thin, you're going to have lots of vague acquaintances and very few real relationships. Focus on those that will be fulfilling and beneficial. Don't only pursue people inside your company either. You may find that customers, people outside the company, or people in your network have a lot to offer.

There are other ways to form relationships than taking people to lunch, playing golf, or sharing drinks at the local watering hole. Some of that still works, but today bonds seem to form more through an information exchange process; tell someone you'd like to get to know about a great article you just read which pertains to what they're doing, or contribute an idea that will help them meet a challenge that got brought up at a meeting. Don't be a flake—if you say you're going to do something, do it, or have a very good reason why you can't. Relationships are formed on mutual respect and trust. People need to know you're going to do what you say you're going to do.

Last, take a work relationship inventory every ninety days and evaluate it. Who are my relationships with? How are they doing? What do I need to do to improve them? Are any of the people Draculas? Be careful: They're sometimes hard to recognize because it's (initially, anyway) flattering to be wanted and needed. You want to be continually reviewing all aspects of your relationships and separating the wheat from the chaff.

Soft Skills

Soft skills are those not related to your education or work experience. There was a time when employers were only interested in knowing about your work experience and your college degree, but while they are still important, your soft skills are what's paramount now.

In order to move our careers forward we need to learn how to prove that our education and experience (regardless of whether it's in the same industry) has prepared us for the challenges of tomorrow's workplace, and specifically, the challenges that face our company or our industry.

A great example of a person who understood the value of his soft skills is Lou Gerstner, the man who turned IBM around when it was in a downward spiral. Although he certainly had a lot of experience running companies, he did not come from a technology background, and did not have a degree from M.I.T. (he's a Harvard MBA guy). What he did have was a wealth of soft skills (see below) and the ability to get things done in the face of considerable resistance.

Lou Gerstner had three specific soft skills which everyone should try to develop:

Problem-solving skills. You have to be results oriented, creative, and proactive. Companies are looking for problem solvers, regardless of your degree (or lack of it), or your experience.

People skills. You also have to be able to get along with your teammates, your customers, and your network. Tolerance is one people skill which is particularly crucial to learn, though difficult for many of us who tend to be perfectionists. It's vital that you learn to allow people to make mistakes, allow (encourage even) people to take chances. The companies with the best track records, the ones who have developed breakthrough products and services, are often those who push their people to take risks and to think outside the box.

Integrated skills. Believe it or not, every new generation of software affects what you do. You need to understand how what's going on in the technical world will impact your industry. Will it help speed up communications with your clients? Will it replace the current accounting practices you use? Which jobs will be impacted? Good example of an industry that ignored how technology would impact their business is the newspaper industry. For decades that business counted on help wanted ads to bring in the majority of their revenues. They didn't see this entire on-line job-board industry (*monster.com*) until they were way behind the eight ball. Consequently, they lost at least a third of their client base. Moral of the story: Be diligent about integrating technology into the way you interface and communicate with team members, fellow workers, and customers.

Get Unstuck

Stuck in the same old rut? A very smart guy once said that the only difference between a rut and the grave is a matter of depth. Is the company crushing the life out of your future? Do you feel that your boss is ignoring your accomplishments? Though we tend to point the finger at somebody or something else as the cause of our malaise at work, most often I've found it's an inside job.

Start getting unstuck by making a list of all the things you've been procrastinating, whether at work or at home. Then methodically eliminate every item on the list, one by one. *E-v-e-r-y* item. All of them. Start clean.

Once you've unburdened yourself, try to avoid getting backlogged again. The best way is to let all the players in your life (spouses, friends, coworkers, kids, *everybody*) know what the boundaries are—what they can ask of you and when they can ask. Explain that if you take on too many tasks, chances are you won't get any of them done so you have to be selective about what you agree to do for people. Everyone will understand, and they'll all appreciate the happier, more productive *you* that emerges.

Ask friends (close friends only) what they think your strengths are and find ways to make them visible. You know what to do: identify your strengths and make changes to allow them to flourish. If I had a great head of hair, I wouldn't wear a hat all the time. Neither should you. If your backhand's weak, play to your forehand.

Make an agreement with yourself not to tolerate negative influences in your life, whether it's a Dracula type of relationship or somebody who relishes in criticizing you. Don't tolerate it. You can invite them out of your life. Sometimes you'll be able to do it politely, sometimes not. But do it.

Type this up and put it on your bathroom mirror: GO CONFIDENTLY IN THE DIRECTION OF YOUR DREAM.

Be Seen as a Leader

You don't have to aim for CEO or VP of Operations, but in your work world, whether it be accounting, construction, or secretarial, be seen as a leader. There are a number of ways to achieve this.

Make sure that you are known as someone with integrity. No, you don't have to achieve godly heights of rectitude, but you want to be identified as someone who always tries to do the right thing.

Have a strong work ethic. Having a strong work ethic does *not* mean working twenty hours a day. That's just dumb. But if you do the best you can to be the best you can and give every job a hundred percent effort, you'll be seen as a leader. Remember, though, that you can be seen as a leader (and perhaps more so) if you have work/life balance.

The ability to handle failure is another sign of leadership. If you blow up and scream at everybody in the vicinity when a project goes south, nobody will mistake you for a leader. A great example of leadership is Joe Torre, manager of the New York Yankees. Listening to him after a game, it's hard to tell if they won or lost; he's very even tempered about it. He understands that the best teams, the best players, fail from time to time. Getting excited, berating the players and placing blame doesn't help the situation. The owner of the Yankees, George Steinbrenner, is slowly, very slowly, learning this valuable lesson. I hope.

Leaders are straight talkers, so say what's on your mind, not what you think people want to hear or the party line of the week.

Be willing to make the tough (and sometimes unpopular) decisions.

Learn to focus and prioritize. Being able to cut through the smoke screen, identify your goal, then prioritize the steps to get there is an invaluable leadership quality.

If you act as a leader, you will be seen as a leader, treated as a leader, and very soon be a leader. The workplace (and certainly the world) needs leaders. Be one.

Specializing in Solutions

If you've read this book (really read it), you know that companies of the future are going to be looking for people who can solve problems. You, naturally, want to be known as someone who specializes in solutions.

First, become an expert at acquiring information. You should be someone whom people can count on to always have a wealth of information on your industry, your company, or your particular project.

Think outside the box. More and more, you'll find that few of the old bromides don't apply in today's workplace. The best solutions in business today often come from people who are willing to look through a different lens than everybody else, people willing to experiment (and possibly fail), people unafraid of trying something new.

Study problems from all points of view. Examine them from left field, from right field, from behind the plate, and maybe from a seat high in the stands where a customer might be. Ask people you respect for insight, regardless of whether they have a background in the issue you're trying to address. They can often give clearer, unobstructed, unencumbered views that will find the solution quicker than those of us too close to the fire.

Don't be afraid to rely on your intuition. A lot of technology people are uncomfortable with this, but the older I get, the more confident I've become in listening to that still, small voice niggling the back of my brain.

Even great problem solvers make mistakes from time to time; it comes with the territory. If you leave the ball game the first time you screw up, make a bad call, or strike out, you'll never make the late innings.

Get Comfortable with Technology

There are still many of us who are not comfortable with technology. We don't know how to use it, don't know what part it plays in our careers, and every time the subject comes up, we look across the room and develop that thousand-yard stare. *What, me worry?* I was that way until a few years ago when I began to realize what technology could do for me. To be able to attach a document to an e-mail, send it across the country, and in five seconds flat have it in the recipient's hands—that's what I call progress.

Know what you want to be good at. Do you want to be an expert in e-mail communication? Do you want to be a spreadsheet whiz? Develop a broad background with several specialties that will allow you to interact with the majority of the working world? Once you have figured out what you want to be good at, you must determine the proper technology that will help you toward the end game.

Spend time with software people, talk to the experts, find out what's going to be best for your career goals. It's more important to understand software than hardware (unless you're a computer tech). Hardware is the delivery system but what they're delivering is much more important to you. Talk to people in your field and find out what software they're using, how they like it, and if they had to do it over again, would they choose the same software.

Make a technology buddy, someone you can trade information with. The world of the future is going to be technology based. All of it. I find it frustrating today to deal with people who don't have e-mail addresses. Or a fax machine. Get current and stay current, or else I guarantee you'll be left behind.

Become Customer-centric

People like Tom Peters (*In Search of Excellence*) and Harry Dent, Jr. (*The Roaring 2000s*), who have researched the workplace, all agree that one of the great breakthroughs coming out of the technology revolution is that we're going to become much more customer-centric. The successful companies of today and tomorrow are willing to adapt themselves, in almost any way, to what the customer wants.

Today's consumer is faced with a broad choice of very good products. Is a BMW better than a Mercedes? An HP better than a Compaq? A Kenmore better than a Whirlpool? It's the company that has a good product, good customer service and support, and that makes it easy for me to buy, that is probably going to get my business.

Dell Computers is a great example of a company that knows how to adapt to what the customer wants. Not so long ago, if you wanted a computer, you went into a store, talked to a few salespeople who knew (in many cases) little more than you did, and then you bought something off the shelf which may or may not have been equipped the way you really wanted it. You had to be satisfied with "good enough." Dell was the one that raised the bar. They created a business plan that catered to what the customer wanted. Not that that concept was new, it's just that there weren't very many companies actually "walking the walk" and delivering real customer service. The big differentiator in Dell's model was they figured out that they could give their clients what they wanted by changing their internal decision-making processes. It worked. Today, you can call Dell, tell them how much memory you want, what kind of hard drive, what kind of CD Rom you prefer, and they'll deliver it tomorrow. *That's* customer service.

All of us in the workplace are, to some degree, involved with the customer. Whether you're a waiter, a truck driver, or a mail clerk, you need to think customer-centrically (hey, new word!). One of the predictions of job futurists is that as much as 50 percent of us will move to what they call the front line, dealing with customers directly on a day to day basis. Companies are removing the layers they used to have in their bureaucracies so that people on the front line are empowered to respond to customer needs on a one to one basis. Once again, Dell is a good example of forward-thinking policies. Most of the people in Dell's customer service and technical support can make decisions on the spot; they don't have to run a customer's request up the ladder and get a command decision. And that's one of the reasons they're such a dominant force in the marketplace. Their model of giving their customer what they want, on the spot, has resulted in unparalleled sales and profit growth in their industry.

You need to be the kind of person who's willing to make on-the-spot decisions. In my former worklife, it was always very frustrating for me when I couldn't solve a customer's problem immediately, when I had to go through a layer or two of management to get a decision or approval. Even after I did solve the problem, I knew that I had robbed the customer of one of his most important assets—time. We need to take the attitude that what's best for the customer is often what's best for the company. The simple equation is, *no customers equals no company.* So treat them well; without them you're nothing.

I hate to repeat myself, but here I go again: You need to be adaptable. A wise Roman (or Greek maybe) said "All is changing save the law of change" a couple of centuries ago. It's still true today. One day you're a project team leader. The next day you are the person leading a sales presentation. The third day, you're writing copy for your company's Web site. You won't play the same role every day. You'll do what needs to be done that day, often dictated by your clients. Customers change. We change. The market changes. The company changes. This is why it's so important to be project oriented.

Consider getting another degree, become an expert in a crucial bit of software, master the language of the country where the company just opened the newest branch, anything to make yourself indispensable to the company. If you've seen Bob Dylan's band recently, you know that the lead guitar not only plays a great lead, he also plays a pedal steel and a fiddle. The ability to fulfill more than one role may well have landed him the job of touring with Dylan. If success like that isn't worth a couple of night school classes, I don't know what is. Obviously, you may not end up touring with Dylan, but the lesson is the same—be adaptable.

Be Somebody

This is a hard one for a lot of us. Seems like we always want to be somebody special, famous, larger-than-life, a movie star, rock star, or sports star. The truth is that we all have the ability to be somebody greater than who we are today. For twenty-five years I thought of myself as a sales manager or general manager type. It didn't occur to me that I could be anything else. Why should it? I had talent for that kind of work, and enjoyed success in those arenas. But once I became comfortable with the idea that I didn't have to do sales, in fact, I could branch out into something totally different and exciting, the barriers that I had set up began tumbling down. (Take note: the barriers were those *I* had set up.) No, I didn't become a rock star (because I can't sing and I quit taking piano lessons when I was seven), or a basketball star (I'd need a tall ladder to be able to dunk), but I did become an author and a career coach. And I've never been happier.

Raise the bar. Decide that you're going to be somebody, do something different, engage life in a different way, expect more of yourself. You don't have to accept mediocrity. A great line in Richard Bach's *Illusions* says, "Argue for your limitations and they're yours." You don't have to be a checker in a grocery store (unless you want to be—and that's fine, too.) Aim high—you probably won't become a bank president next week, but if you raise the bar a bit at a time, you'll be surprised at how high you can jump.

I tell my clients to think two levels ahead. If you're trying to move your career forward, think not only about next week, but next year as well. Imagine you're playing a chess game. You only move one piece at a time, but if you're a good chess player, you're thinking at least two moves ahead, and they're all contingent on what your opponent does. Knight to bishop four may work unless . . . unless . . . Be prepared with a countermove. If you know the opposition (the business world) and understand the current job market, you're prepared to make some killer moves.

Invest in self-training. If your excuse is lack of time or money, all I can say is, get the money and find the time. It's your career and your life. If not now, when? Some training will cost money, but there's a lot of it on the Internet that's pretty inexpensive. Check out *ask.com*, type in on-line training, to see what I mean. Don't have a computer or Internet access? Go down to the local library and use theirs. Take classes. Buy books (lots of used ones out there). If you're sitting still, you're actually going backward.

What are you best at? Though you've got to be flexible and adaptable, you want to identify your real core competency. Red Adair (is he still around?) used to put out oil field fires, and that's what he became known for. He could be a concert violinist for all I know; what he's become known as is a guy who can put out oil field fires better than anyone else. Period. What can you do?

Finally, be able to work well with others. If you look at people who have been successful, you'll find that most of them know how to go along to get along. If you're ever going to get a Get Stuff Done degree, working well with others is an absolute prerequisite. You'll find out (if you haven't already) that you sometimes need help to get stuff done. Since the best somebody to be is a somebody who can get stuff done, you darn well better know how to ask for, and offer, help. I don't care if you drive a trash truck, paint houses, or you're the chairman of the board, if you don't learn to work well with others, you'll never have the kind of success you deserve.

You're not limited by your past experience, nor limited by your degree or lack of it; being somebody is a decision. Your decision. Take the time and energy to explore the possibilities.

Chapter Twelve: Exercises

EXERCISE 1 Raising the Bar on Your Career

One of the most exciting aspects of career coaching is the challenge. If you have a good coach, some of his challenges will make your chin drop to your knees as you plead, "I can't do that!" It's rather like when your dad took the training wheels off your bike. At that time, his idea that you could ride without them seemed impossible. But he knew something you didn't: that you were capable of balancing without them, and the only way to develop the skill was to practice, fall off a few times, and keep getting back on.

Career coaches are effective for many of the same reasons. They refuse to buy into your self-imposed limitations. They see more potential for greatness in you than you see in yourself.

So in the spirit of raising the bar on your career, here's a series of outrageous challenges for you. Take on a few, and you'll find yourself playing a bigger game.

There are three acceptable responses to a coach's challenge:

1. **"Yes, I accept the challenge."** Write down what you will do in your calendar. Commit to it. Get into action, and try not to think too much about it.

2. **"No, I refuse the challenge."** Valid response: No one is holding a gun to your head. But you might want to look at why you're saying no. Write down all the logical, rational reasons for saying no, and then (gulp) take a peek underneath these reasons and write down what you're *really* afraid of. Be ruthlessly honest with yourself. You might also check in and see if your critic had anything to do with the decision to reject the challenge (see Chapter 6).

3. **"I want to renegotiate some of the terms of the challenge."** Renegotiate all you want, but don't lower the bar too far. If you can come up with an assignment that makes you gulp, that's perfect. By all means avoid the challenges that make you go weak at the knees!

EXERCISE 2 The Challenges

1. Use at least three consecutive personal or vacation days to reassess your career, do some of the exercises in this book, and take a 30,000-foot view of your life. Don't try doing it when you're rushing around and overwhelmed. Make some space for yourself.

2. By the end of the next working day, create or join a project at work. Practice the skill of completion by getting your part of the project done at least

50 percent ahead of schedule. Then give the credit for your success to someone else.

3. End a relationship with an energy vampire at work. This can mean having a polite boundary setting conversation, or simply agreeing inwardly not to give any more energy to that relationship. Commit to it absolutely.

BONUS CHALLENGE: *Identify three energy drains in your life as a whole, and give them up. Start by lending your television to a friend for a month.*

4. Identify a person in your network who you don't know real well, but with whom you feel energized and positive. Find and e-mail them an article relevant to their industry or interests, and invite them to lunch at the same time.

5. Find **five** separate sources of information about your industry, and trends in your geographic region. Write on your schedule when you will spend time with each one, committing to complete all five in the next month. Over the course of this month, send no less than **ten** articles to people in your network.

6. Create a portfolio of your problem-solving skills, people skills, and integrated skills. Come up with a way of representing each (case studies, testimonials, reports of your past successes, awards and comments on your performance evaluations). Assemble them into a document of no more than three pages, emphasizing your biggest wins. Make it look sharp and professional.

7. Make a list of areas where you've been procrastinating. Cross five items off your list right now (you know the ones you think you *should* do, will never want to do, and will never get around to). Why hold on to them?

8. With the remaining items on your procrastination list, write them into your calendar in such a way that they will be complete within seven days. Take vacation time if you need to. Refuse to allow yourself to start any new projects until you're caught up. Hint for hard-core Ph.D. procrastinators: Try talking yourself into it rather than talking yourself out of it.

9. Make eight deposits per day into your integrity bank. That is, keep your word, or apologize for not doing so.

10. Identify an area of your life (doesn't have to be career) where you've not spoken up directly and honestly. Pick up the phone *right now* and clean it up. Ask if it's a good time for the other person involved, and then say what you have to say. Yes, the challenge is to do it now. *Carpe diem.*

11. Identify an area of your professional life where you have a long-standing complaint. Write down how you see it. Then practice thinking outside of

the box by imagining how else you could look at it. Try on the point of view of the following people: a five-year-old, your mother, a paranoid person, your guardian angel, O. J. Simpson's legal team, and the Pope.

12. Choose a twenty-four-hour period to get to know your intuition. Write it on your calendar. During that day, pay attention to every random thought, impression, and instinct, particularly the ones which nag at you. Act on at least three. See how you feel at the end of the day.

13. Open a piece of software you use every day at work. Find three features you've never used before, and using the help system, friends, and online resources, learn how to use them. Then use each feature at least once in the next seven days.

14. Make an on-the-spot decision today that makes a customer happy. Don't give away the farm, but think about the situation from your customer's point of view.

15. Identify an additional skill which would make you more valuable to your employer. If you don't know what that would be, ask your employer to tell you. Then get on the Web, or open your local newspaper or even the Yellow Pages, and find a class that can teach it. Do whatever you need to do to find the money and the time, and sign up.

16. What self-imposed limitations hold back your career? Write down a list of at least twenty things you can't do, using sentences beginning with the words, "I can't . . ." Then rewrite the list, starting each sentence with, "I choose not to . . ." or "I haven't yet learned to . . ." Choose one item on the list, and do whatever it takes to be able to say, "I can!"

Some Tips for the Bosses

O ur previous twelve chapters have been about the workers, how they can cope with all the imminent changes in the workplace, how they can not only survive, but actually prosper in a rapidly changing business market. This chapter is for the bosses, how they need to understand who today's worker is, and how he/she differs from the employee of only a few short years ago. So here are a few suggestions on how bosses can be better managers and better stewards of the highly skilled and mobile workforce of the new millennium.

What Workers Want

A number of recent studies indicate that what employees want is sometimes strikingly (pardon the pun) different from what bosses think they want. Obviously a dicey situation. Here are some of the main concerns workers generally address, not necessarily in order of importance.

#1 Workers want flexible hours. According to a recent *Chicago Tribune* survey, some 38 percent of us do.

#2 They want to be able to telecommute. According to that earlier referenced American Management Association study, companies that allow flexible hours and some telecommuting report, on average, higher productivity than companies that don't. It is working. Companies that find a way to provide it will benefit.

#3 On-site child care. The days of the two person household where one stays home and the other provides the income are pretty much gone. There are single moms out there, many of them excellent in their field. Companies that provide day care will find it easier to attract the best talent from this ever-growing pool.

#4 Tuition reimbursement. Training is important (although my studies show not as important as it once was). Employees feel that you're investing in them when you support their decision to take personal time to pursue an educational path that will benefit the company.

#5 They want a say in the company vision and direction. There was a time when the president of the company seemed to have the sole responsibility for company direction. He disappeared into The Office, thought Big Thoughts about Things, maybe took some (perhaps illegal) substance, and had a vision. Then he told everyone what it was in a speech, or, more often, in a memo. Ultimately, though, if it was a vision that few shared, it wasn't likely to get off the ground. Most workers understand that they're not going to decide if the company should stop making a certain product or discontinue a service. My suggestion to bosses, however, is that you allow workers an input into the system; you may be surprised at what they come up with. Some of the best ideas at companies I've worked for have come from lower echelon employees.

#6 They want the ability to challenge the company. Forget suggestion boxes—most workers realize that companies don't take suggestion boxes very seriously. If they see something wrong, something that can be done better, they want to be able to challenge old policies and say, "Here's a way we can do this better." They don't want to be chastised for speaking up, and they don't want to feel that they're not taken seriously. Employees should be able to confront their boss or company about issues, particularly if they have some possible solutions to go along with their concerns. The best companies actually have channels set up for those employees who want to express their views but want to remain anonymous.

#7 Workers want interesting assignments. A few years ago corporate America started something called cross-functional training, which has had some significant impact on the workers. For whatever reason (and maybe you can blame TV or video games or computers), today's workforce wants interesting, challenging assignments. This is another way of saying we seem to get bored easily. Good thing? Bad thing? Maybe a little of each, but what seems to be a fact is that we're less likely to want to do repetitive tasks. Top performing companies have figured out ways, with the help of their employees, to spread the grunt work around so that the same few people don't get stuck doing it every day. The result is everyone feeling like they are an important part of the team.

#8 They want a sense of purpose at work. More and more employees are looking for meaning in what they do, not just a contribution to the bottom line. Let them know how their efforts are valuable to the company, how their work improves the quality of your product.

#9 Workers want to be happy at work. (Remember the happy meter?) They want to have more fun. People are willing to work hard and contribute time, energy, and skill to their companies, but they also want to be happy doing it. All work and no play makes for low morale and a sluggish work environment. So host a company picnic, initiate Take Your Kid to Work Day, organize company softball teams. You'll see immediate improvements.

The Key Work Traits of Highly Effective Bosses

When I ask my clients what qualities they want in a boss, I usually get the same answers. Good bosses are:

#1 Honest. Workers want bosses who tell the truth, no matter how painful it might be to hear. You are better off laying the cards on the table, even if the news is not particularly good.

#2 Able to function well in a changing environment. Bosses need to embrace change, too, maybe even more than the employees. If you embrace change as a challenge, those who work for you will also. Here's an example: Our company, Delta Road, had to figure out how to contract 100 new people within thirty days. We had never done it before. But the team took it as a challenge, got together as a group, and figured out how to make it happen. We landed 107 people in twenty-nine days.

#3 Respectful. Whether you're dealing with another boss, a coworker, a subordinate (shouldn't we do away with that word?), or someone who works for a rival company, you should never belittle other people, especially if your job is to manage or oversee them. No exceptions. I'm not saying that it's easy to do. But you owe it to yourself not to walk around having an attitude about someone's behavior. It doesn't help anyone. I suggest you take the person you are having a problem with out to coffee to discuss your concerns. Relate to them in a way that doesn't attack the person, but to how it is impacting the team or company negatively. More often than not the person will thank you for the feedback and try to do something about it. If they don't understand what you're saying, try to accept it and move on.

#4 Able to make tough decisions quickly. The operative word is "quickly." Make your decision, stand by it, and be willing to answer questions about why you made it. You don't have to give a one-hour dissertation to everyone who asks, but you should be able to give a reason (or reasons) why you made it. When you get the reputation as someone who is willing to take a calculated risk, make a decision quickly, and change it if necessary, your value to the company will go up exponentially.

#5 Able to keep their commitments. Everybody understands that there may be times when you can't live up to every promise you make. The business environment may change drastically, the company may need to switch directions for any number of reasons, or upper management may have a collective ulcer attack that leads to another reorganization. But what workers want to see is that their bosses make every possible effort to keep the commitments they make; and if they can't, that they're willing to sit down and explain why not. Workers will respect you if you treat their concerns, and their feelings, like they matter. Your employees might be a little (or extremely) irritated at the time you make your confession, but in the long run, you'll gain more followers than adversaries by being up-front and sincere.

#6 People who have rock-solid integrity. Being totally honest is vital to your image, but integrity is the jewel in the crown. The boss doesn't have to be perfect, but he or she should live by a strict code of ethics.

#7 People with a superior work ethic. Bosses who routinely work twelve to fourteen hours a day may think they are setting a good example, but most workers don't respect that kind of masochism. They want to see that you have a life outside the Hallowed Halls of Business, want to know that you think family is important, that exercise is important, that leisure time is important, because if they aspire to be the boss someday themselves, they don't want to be stuck in the same dungeon twelve to fourteen hours a day with no other life. You must lead by example.

#8 Able to handle failure. Practically everyone's had one—a boss who goes ballistic when something doesn't go right. Employees don't want to work for someone who turns into Mr. Hyde or Cruella De Vil when their plans don't run as smoothly as they expected. No one will fault you for showing disappointment or admitting frustration, but temper tantrums are unacceptable. People working for you will take their lead from your reactions. If you have a temper tantrum, it gives them leave to have one too. Plus, it's a sure-fire precursor to your team developing a morale problem. You're a leader. Act like one.

#9 Able to focus and prioritize. Everyone needs to do this, but it is vital for bosses. Be flexible, be able to navigate as needed, stay focused on the end game and prioritize accordingly.

Why Smaller Companies Are Beating Out the Competition for the Best Talent

Given the tight market, it's difficult for companies to hire and retain the best people. But the trend right now is that it's the *smaller* companies that are hiring and keeping the best people in the market. Traditionally, top candidates chose to work for bigger companies because they felt they were offered more stability, better benefits, and better opportunities to advance. Due to the changes in the marketplace and the workforce itself, that's no longer necessarily the case: Statistics show that the larger percentage of layoffs stem from the bigger companies. So much for stability.

Today's workforce tends to be more entrepreneurial than ever before, and job hunters see smaller companies as more fertile ground for their career goals. This is not to say that there aren't some big companies out there—Microsoft, Dell Computers, Sun, and others—where a person can make a name for themselves and professionally skyrocket. What's interesting, though, is that part of what makes them so successful is that they think, and more often than not act, like small businesses.

Why are smaller companies winning the battle for the best people? I thought you'd never ask.

#1 They let people make decisions on the spot. Small companies don't have a choice but to let people think for themselves and use their judgment. Without the eighteen layers of management common to big companies, those who are on the front lines have to make front line decisions. So if you run a small company, you'd better make it your mission to have good people there. In his book *The Roaring 2000s,* Harry Dent predicts that the network organization of the future is going to put as much as 50 percent of the workforce on the front line and give them decision-making capabilities.

#2 They give employees easy access to top management. Having access to the person at the top gives employees a sense of closeness with the company itself. Long, long ago, when Hewlett-Packard was actually a small company, Hewlett and Packard wandered around the manufacturing divisions and the sales offices on a regular basis. And, I am told on good authority, that they never allowed anyone to address them as "Mister." It was always Dave and Bill. Their actions helped reduce the invisible barrier between the ranks and promote a sense of "we are all in this together." It obviously worked!

#3 Employees of smaller companies generally feel that they are making a difference. And that's because they actually are. Each individual counts for a lot more than in a big company, where there's more machinery and it's harder to see how each part contributes to the whole. There is kind of a faceless anonymity inherent in large corporations. Small companies encourage each person to achieve a sense of purpose, of being a useful contributor to a greater cause.

#4 They are more likely to have performance-based compensation. Although there are still lots of people who want the old steady paycheck every week or two, more and more of us want to be involved and have our compensation based on how well we perform. We want some skin in the game. I want to help this company, but they need to be willing to put more in my paycheck if I perform as advertised. This system could result in lots more money in my paycheck, depending on how well I do. Well, that's a position of strength for me since I now can have a real impact on how much money I make. If I work smarter, make great decisions, make things happen, I can make more moola. I know I can do something to boost my bottom line.

#5 They have a tendency to be more flexible. Flextime, telecommuting, hey, we like all that stuff. Smaller companies typically can better accommodate alternative schedules because they aren't so bureaucratic, tied to policies and procedures like big companies. They seem to be in a better position to roll with the punches.

#6 They typically do a better job of encouraging new ideas. Nuff said.

#7 They have a more positive, rewarding culture. It's hard for many people to feel attached to or part of a big company. Consequently, the culture that develops tends to be very arm's-length, lukewarm at best. Small companies typically provide a better vehicle to have a more positive culture. You can feel the energy the minute you walk through the door.

Random Advice

The best managers of today are not the dictators or tyrants of typical yesteryear (is that an old word, or what?). The old hierarchy of authority is disappearing like the proverbial snowball in August. Today's best managers are facilitators; they are the men and women who create a winning environment, who create a culture that makes people want to come to work every day, who lets employees know that they make a difference, that they have a sense of purpose. They provide the tools (both hard and soft) that make a successful company possible. They create the recipe for success—take ten committed people, add incentive, commitment, environment, condiments, let simmer (or boil as the case may be), serve when ready.

I recently heard of a company that sends out a questionnaire to their employees every month asking for a list of what they call "performance inhibitors." Basically it says, "What are we, as a company, doing that inhibits your ability to do a great job?" It's a terrific idea, though some words of warning: You have to act on some of those suggestions or you will soon find that no one bothers to return the questionnaire.

A high turnover rate is not necessarily the result of poor employee selection. Be aware that sometimes there are other factors. I have a few ideas you might want to try.

Reduce the number of meetings you hold. And when you do have meetings, make them short and to the point, have an agenda, and stick to it. Bosses often think that meetings are the only way to communicate with their departments. Not so. Remember Dave and Bill at Hewlett-Packard? Their management policy was called MBWA—Management By Wandering Around. They tell me it worked very well. You might want to try it.

This next suggestion may raise the hackles on a few bosses. Some companies are connecting management pay (not all of it, but a significant amount) to employee satisfaction. How about that? Are you confident enough in your leadership ability to say, "Okay, a third of my pay will be based on employee satisfaction."? If you are, you're going to be seen as an exceptional leader, one who's probably on the fast track to success.

Designate two (possibly more) people as an inside espionage team. Their job will be to sniff around and find out how other managers keep their turnover rates low. Ideally, what you want to do is apply the best practices to your own enterprise. You can learn from other people's failures, too (who loses people every month?), but the successes will give you more immediate help.

Wherever possible, focus on promise and possibilities. Your employees will rise to the occasion. I'm not saying stick your head in the sand when faced with problems, but don't focus on them. Learn from your mistakes (or the mistakes of others) and move on. You'll create a more positive work environment. An inspirational story about someone who didn't let problems stand in his way is that of Fred Smith, now CEO of FedEx. Back when he was in college, he submitted a paper on his idea, a spoke and hub distribution method which would eventually become what we know as Federal Express. The professor gave Fred a C, commenting on all the problems with the idea, instead of focusing on the promise and possibility it held. Lucky for us Fred had faith in his project and turned it into a multi-billion dollar business (no thanks to his shortsighted professor).

Since you want to keep your turnover rate low, you'll want to make it an absolute priority to improve the talent pool. I saw a recent survey stating that 75 percent of companies out there thought talent (the lack of it) was a big problem. Yet, only 20 percent of them are doing much about it. Make sense? Of course not. An obvious tip: Do something about it. Make it a major initiative within your company to not only hire better talent, but also to build the kind of culture within your firm that makes you an employer of choice, that is, the kind of company people want to work for and stay working for.

Though generally you want to do what you can to get people to stay, there will be times when you're happy to see someone go. Don't tolerate bad employees. If you've got discontented employees, sour apples, troublemakers, whatever you call them, the first thing you should do is try to turn them into valuable employees. It sometimes works and can be well worth the effort. If it doesn't work, get rid of them; it takes only one or two grumblers to poison the atmosphere. And get rid of them quickly; don't turn them into projects. You'll earn more respect from the other employees, and you'll have more energy to build up those people who *want* to work with you.

If you're thinking about changing a policy or procedure that impacts the company, do it on a pilot project basis. Don't carve your decree onto stone tablets and have someone bring it down from the mountain before you've had a chance to test it out. You'll only build resentment throughout your department.

One of the best ways to keep your staff consistent and happy is to be extra cautious when hiring new talent. During an interview, you might realize you're with someone who almost fits the mold you're looking for, who has all the right credentials, but for whatever reason you're just not sure that they're going to be right for your company. In cases like this, you might want to think about conducting a working interview. Have the job-hopeful come into your department and work for a half day or a day. See how they fit into the group. See if they fit well from a personality standpoint, from a work ethic standpoint, from a vision of what's possible to accomplish standpoint. Take them to lunch, introduce them to people, watch them perform a few tasks. You can tell a lot about a person by watching them in a group setting for a few hours.

The CEO of *Amazon.com* is a man named Jeff Bezos. He has implemented a hiring philosophy that focuses not so much on education and experience, but on other factors that he thinks are more important. The prospective hire is interviewed by a number of people in the department, then the hiring managers get together and focus on what they admire. They talk about the candidate's soft skills, characteristics, traits; is the person involved in the community, do they do volunteer work, are they active in a civic organization? What they've found is that the best workers are not necessarily those with the best education or the most experience. My suggestion to the bosses out there is to look beyond the simple facts of the résumé, find out about people skills and community commitment; you might find a real jewel carefully hidden underneath all the customary trapping like diplomas and awards.

Sun Microsystems (big, big, big) is so concerned about how hard people are working (evidently people love to work for them) that they hired career counselors to work with employees they felt were working too hard. They called them Get-a-Life Counselors, and their jobs were to counsel people they felt were in danger of becoming workaholics. The old corporate model of pushing people to work long hours, take work home, work on weekends if necessary, only proved that it was possible to burn people out in a very short time. Companies like Sun are teaching us that you can have an extremely productive workforce and still have balance.

Effective management structure is more vital than it's ever been, and some of the old procedures, the old tactics, won't cut it anymore to keep up with the rapidly changing work environment. Good bosses will have to change their ways. The workforce will be increasingly entrepreneurial and bosses will be facilitators (which may be what they should have been all along).

Gentlemen (and -women) . . . start your engines . . .

Chapter Thirteen: Exercises

EXERCISE 1 Tips for the Bosses

This section is written specifically for managers, but it's relevant for anyone in the workplace, no matter what your current level. If you're not in a managerial or leadership role now, these exercises can help you be effective when you get there, if that's on your career map. Also, if you like the picture of twenty-first-century workplace leadership that we've painted in this chapter, you might consider buying a copy of this book for your boss . . .

Research and Inquiry:
What do you think your employees want?

- Write down your perceptions, and then interview a sample of at least five people in your company.

- Do the two lists compare? Are you out of touch with what your employees want, or are you in synch? Note any differences between what you would want as an employee, and what your employees are telling you: If a benefit or practice wouldn't appeal to you, then it is most likely to reside in your "blind spot."

College Flashback:
Write a personal response to the following statement.
"As a senior manager, I have two distinct sets of customers. The first are the people who buy our services. The second are my employees. If I treat both my employees and customers with the same respect, listening, support, and understanding of their critical importance in executing my business plan, I cannot fail."

Brainstorming: Creating an environment which gives workers what they want.

- Review the following list of employee goals. Add any that you found from your own interviews.

- When filling out the chart below, let go of considerations of what's possible, reasonable, affordable, and traditionally a part of your company's culture. Make this an exercise in thinking outside the box, and give yourself permission to use your imagination. You can always assess viability later.

EMPLOYEE GOAL	WHAT I COULD DO TO MAKE IT HAPPEN	WHAT THE COMPANY COULD DO TO MAKE IT HAPPEN	WHAT INDIVIDUAL EMPLOYEES COULD DO TO MAKE IT HAPPEN
Flexible hours			
Telecommuting			
On-site child care			
Tuition reimbursement			
A say in company vision and direction			
The ability to challenge the company			
Interesting assignments			
A sense of purpose at work			
To be happy at work			

Action: Once you've filled up the grid with ideas and options, it's time to create a three-part action plan.

Part One: What I will do, when I will do it, what outcome I intend.

Part Two: Evaluate each item for feasibility, budgetary implications, and value returned to the organization as a result. Turn the three most promising ideas into proposals. Ask for feedback from colleagues, employees, and individuals with expertise in the HR/OD (organizational development) area.

Part Three: Do employees know what they could do to get what they want? What communication, coaching, and training needs to happen for employees to take responsibility for these elements?

Sales Pitch Interlude

If you're interested in turning your company into an employer of choice, you need to know about Delta Road *(www.deltaroad.com)*. Delta Road is the largest national community of corporate and career coaches, and this is exactly the area corporate coaching can address. Corporate coaching works directly to support companies in developing employee-centered management practices, and supporting individual employees in taking full responsibility for their career satisfaction. This process can make a tremendous difference for companies in their efforts to retain and develop their top talent.

Exercise:

Evaluate your current management practices, using a scale of 1 to 10. Be ruthlessly honest with yourself, but don't allow your critic to answer these questions for you! This exercise can show you the "growing edge" of your development as a leader.

9–10 = I have achieved mastery in this area. This is one of my core competencies, and a foundation of my success.

7–8 = This area is solid for me. I'm consistent, and my skills in this area have been recognized by others.

5–6 = I do this well sometimes, but I'm erratic. This skill is available to me, but not used to maximum effectiveness.

3–4 = I'm aware of the importance of this, but I forget or choose not to do it, and I can see where that limits my effectiveness.

1–2 = I basically suck in this area. The word "clueless" comes to mind.

_____ Honest

_____ Able to function well in a changing environment

_____ Respectful

_____ Able to make tough decisions quickly

_____ Able to keep my commitments

_____ Rock-solid integrity

_____ A superior work ethic

_____ Able to handle failure

_____ Able to focus and prioritize

Assignment:

For each area which you rate less than a 7, come up with three specific, measurable actions that would raise your score by two points. Retake this test once you have completed those actions.

COACH'S HINT: *If you can't think of ways to improve in an area in which you're weak, or your efforts don't yield the desired results, this is a great time to hire a coach. Probably the most effective path is to hire a professional career coach who specializes in management and leadership development (we can connect you with just such a coach at www.deltaroad.com). Alternatively, find someone in your network who is strong in this area, and interview them. Get to know their perspective, their actions, and their feelings about this aspect of leadership, and try them out for yourself for a week or two.*

Take Your Career On-Line

So here I am, one of the ten most nontechnical people on the planet (I was even worse four or five years ago), and I'm on the Internet at least two or three hours a day, some days even more. Part of that is because it's my job to stay current, to stay informed about everything because everything affects the job market. Though lots of people use the Internet for a variety of reasons, some of the questions I get in my seminars or on my radio program, lead me to believe that most people don't have any idea how powerful the Internet really is. Given that, we're now going to cover the why and how of using the Internet as a tool to advance your career (e.g., job search, write a résumé, find out what your value is in the market place, and explore the job market in, say, Pocatello).

There was a time when the job market could be summarized in

a few simple statements. Get your education (preferably a degree) in your chosen field, find the most stable company (security being the coin of the realm), go to work, put in the years, get cost-of-living raises and an occasional promotion, then retire on a small pension and (if you're lucky) social security benefits. I know I've made the point ad nauseum, but here it is again:

THE TIMES HAVE CHANGED

Here's a little history about searching for careers on-line. The concept didn't even get started until 1994, when a job search site called *careermosaic* began by developing a way for companies to post job openings and giving candidates an opportunity to look at them. That was just a few short years ago. It was kind of a specialty site that didn't get a lot of hits. Then about a year after that, *monsterboard* got started. It was an offshoot started by an advertising agency executive who had been approached by a company saying, "I need you to create a monster recruiting ad on the Internet." As a result, this executive, Jeff Taylor, created *monsterboard.com*, which has grown to be a huge on-line job search site (now *monster.com*). And according to an independent survey done by IDC, they get over three million unique visits a month (unique visits are visits to that specific site, not the page to page or link to link visits that normally count as hits). Forrester Research is projecting that the on-line job search/recruiting industry will grow from the $105 million that it was worth in 1998 to $3 billion in revenue in the year 2005. That's a lot of jobs.

So clearly, advancing your career on-line is something you want to explore. It's not the only way; keep in mind the ways we've discussed so far. But lots of companies are doing on-line searches and you don't want to be left standing at the gate.

There's a feeling in the marketplace that, yeah, on-line Internet stuff is good, but it's mostly for computer jocks and techno-nerds. Not true. *Fortune* magazine informed us in the July '99 issue that 65 percent of all on-line job seekers are not engineers or computer professionals. So there. The same article went on to say that, at the time, there were two and a half million résumés posted on the Internet. In January of '98, 17 percent of the Fortune 500 companies were actively recruiting on the Internet. One year later the number was up to 45 percent. So learn how to use it, and how to make it work to your advantage. If you don't have a computer at home, use the one in your local library or your cybercafé. No excuses.

Up to now, finding a job has not been the easiest thing to do (at least for most of us). The search itself is usually equivalent to a full-time job. Of all the clients I've worked with in the last year (and there have been hundreds), the vast majority had not been using the Internet. Why? They didn't think it was a viable tool. Or they didn't know how to use it. Or they thought it would only lead them to technology-based jobs.

NEWS FLASH!!!
The Internet will make your job search a lot easier.

You know the pertinent career information you always had to dig so hard to find? It's all available on the Internet, lots easier and lots faster. You can sit there in your jammies (the one with the feet in them) at 10 P.M., drinking hot chocolate, and find out what your current job will be worth ten years from now. Find out if your compensation package is at, or above, or (God forbid) below the industry average. Will your position be in demand five years from now? If not, what will be the hot careers? ▷

Companies that use the Internet find that it greatly reduces the time spent in hiring people. A recent *Fortune* article states that for companies using the Internet, the average cycle time spent in hiring was reduced from 128 days to forty-five days. Since time equals money, you can see why companies like it.

The Internet is easier, faster, less costly, and keeps you up to date. Remember how I've stressed that research is vital to a successful career? Get on the Internet; the latest and greatest information will be at your fingertips, and you'll have the advantage of knowing what's really going on in your industry.

Question from the person in the back row. Yes, you with the orange hat.

"Well, Gordon, if the job market is so great, the economy so good, and the labor market so tight, why do I have to go on-line to check out the jobs?"

Good question. Statistics quoted in *Fortune* magazine say that within three to five years, classified ads in the newspapers as we know them are going to disappear. Poof! No more want ads. Get used to not looking there. Instead . . . Right; they'll be replaced by on-line recruiting. Besides (did we say this before?) the best candidates aren't the ones thumbing through the want ads. You shouldn't be either. And by the way, get rid of that orange hat. It doesn't go with your hair.

Here's a list of some of the top ten on-line job Web sites (based on visits per month) you should try:

Monster.com

Careermag.com

Flipdog.com

Jobs.com

HeadHunter.net

NationJob.com

HotJobs.com

Brainbench.com

Dice.com

CareerBuilder.com

Those are the top ten, but there are another thousand sites out there doing on-line recruiting, job search, career advancement, etc. All are obviously smaller, most catering to a specific industry or niche market. For example, there's a site for just nurses in the San Diego area. Maybe that doesn't help you if you live in Fargo (unless you want to move), but it's just the ticket for you Californians.

Here's a random list of some other sites, just to give you an idea of how specialized some of them are:

6figurejobs.com

Collegegrad.com

Christianjobs.com

Bilingualjobs.com

Coloradojobs.com

Casinocareers.com

Blackengineers.org

. . . To name just a few.

The combined total of unique visits per month to job sites is estimated to be twenty-five million. And it's expected to grow.

As for job availability, it's estimated that (as of January 2001), when you consider all the sites, there are fifteen million job postings. As I said, those are not just for tech jobs. There are white-collar jobs, blue-collar jobs, permanent, temporary, sales, PR, accounting, banking, teaching, restaurant workers, take your pick. Very diverse. Go on-line and take a look. Want to change careers? Want to see what's available? Need I say more?

More people today are changing jobs because they want to, not because they have to. Even though there's a tight labor market, there's still heavy competition because people are changing jobs much more often.

As I mentioned earlier in the book, you should always be looking for the next opportunity. Always. I call this "passive job hunting." Even though you absolutely love your job and your company, who knows what the morrow may bring (sounds Shakespearean, doesn't it)? The merger monster may attack without warning; a silent acquisition may have been signed at the midnight hour when you were safely tucked in bed; the morrow may bring sorrow (Hey, maybe I could write plays. Or even poetry). If, however, you have been doing your passive job hunting, you will know where all the life preservers and survival tools are stashed and you will be well away from the current vessel when it sinks. And not only "well away," but on your way to another, presumably better, assignment.

The Internet is the perfect tool for passive job hunting. In the privacy of your own home you can open a window to the whole job world (and other worlds) and find out who's hiring, what they're paying, what the prospects look like long term and short term.

It's a little like fishing. One day you drop the line in the water, troll for a while and see what you get. If nothing comes up, it's not a big deal. You go back the next day or next week or next month and try again. If you latch on to something big, reel it in and take a look at it. It just might be a keeper.

Companies are out there trolling all the time, too. They want to keep an eye on people in the pipeline as possible recruits. If they get a big job contract, they want to be able to beef up their workforce as quickly as possible (you remember—to market, to market, to market we go). Time is money. Market timing is everything. And you want to be positioned to be in the right place, at the right time.

Career advancement tools are also available on the Internet. And there will be more to come. Much more. Our company, Delta Road, has developed a Web site that is all about coaching (big surprise, huh?). *Monster.com* has started a new service that resembles a talent agency auction. They'll allow people to post a variety of interesting details about themselves not normally included in a résumé, and then have companies bid on their services. It's just another indication of how dynamic this on-line thing is becoming.

You can find salary calculators and other indices, and Web sites that will help you determine what's fair compensation in your part of the forest. There's one called the Economic Research Institute, *www.erieri.com* that allows you to type in your occupation and your market, and it will tell you what your job is worth today, what it'll be worth in five years, and even what it will be worth in ten years.

Company profiles are also available. The strong, forward-thinking companies have discovered that they have to let people know what the company culture is like, why they're a great place to work, what the benefits are, and what their vision for the future is. The

Vault.com Web site actually has live interactive exchanges that allow you to go on-line with a company and ask questions. You can see why want ads are going to fade away.

Another thing you'll find available are relocation guides. If you have decided to move, there are sites that will help you find a moving company, help you buy a house, tell you what entertainment costs will be in your new city, and even give you child care options. You can find these sites by going to your home page (Yahoo!, AOL), hitting "search," and asking for a list of relocation sites. Or, you can go to *ask.com*, and ask for the same: relocation sites.

There are a number of sites out there that have career assessment tools available. Again, go to your home page, click on "search," and look for career assessment sites. Or, go to *ask.com*, and (oh, you know the drill). Unhappy where you are? Uncertain about the future of your particular industry? Considering changing fields? Take a look and see how well your skills match with your prospects. This service is a very valuable tool.

Career articles are at your fingertips. You don't have to subscribe to every magazine that comes down the pike with "Business" in the title. Pick your topic and search. You can find what you're looking for in magazines and books and libraries, but why bother when all you have to do is tiptoe into the next room and turn on old reliable HAL? There's immediate access for those of you who are impatient (which, if I'm not mistaken, will probably cover just about everybody reading this book).

Without too much strain, you'll be able to come up with a calendar of job fairs in your area (or around the country). As I told you earlier, I'm a little lukewarm on the whole job fair thing, but I suppose it's useful as a good place to network.

Here's something you should definitely take advantage of. You can now sign up for e-mail notification services on some of these sites and they'll tell you when subjects of interest to you open up. You give them parameters of your ideal position that will include certain things, exclude others, and you've got a small search engine tailored to your needs.

As great as the Web is for finding jobs, information, opportunities, articles, and so forth, it's not a replacement for the other job-hunting techniques and resources we've talked about. It's a tool that enhances your ability to make good (read informed) career choices. If you feel unappreciated, underutilized, ready to move on to greener fields, it's a great tool. If you're a company that's having a tough time finding the right people, it's a great tool. But it's just one tool. If you've only got a hammer in your tool bag, you're not going to be able to fix too many things. So gather screwdrivers, pliers, wrenches, wire cutters, and more. But bring the hammer, too—there just might be a job that calls for one.

For the moment, you won't see many listings on-line for the more traditional professions—lawyers, doctors, clergy, etc. Unfortunately, that's also true for some blue-collar jobs. But I was cruising the Internet the other day and I found listings for dishwashers, convenience store clerks, CEOs, and aerospace engineers, so there are signs that these professions should be catching up to the on-line revolution shortly.

Let's look at the Internet a little more closely from the employer's point of view. As of July '99, there were 15,000 companies recruiting on-line. By 2002, the experts predict that 124,000 businesses will be recruiting on-line. So you can see, this whole on-line job-hunt thing is not a passing fad, but a whole new way to find a job, or for companies to find you. Take it seriously. It works!

One of the things I love about Internet recruiting from a company standpoint is that you can spend a fraction of what you spent on print ads and get a whole page spread on-line with colors and flashing/blinking lights. The whole nine yards. You can even make the page interactive. People can ask questions. Talk to an employee. "Hey, my name's Frank. You like the company you work for? Why?"

One company put out a forty-paragraph document about their company culture, job responsibility, their expectation from new employees, etc. I don't know if I'd recommend that for every company, but certainly variations of it are coming into play every day. But do take advantage of listings like these to find out all you can about the company so you can 1) decide if you really want to work for them and 2) impress the hell out of them with your encyclopedic knowledge of their company.

Andy Grove, chairman of Intel, recently said in *Fast Company*, which in my humble opinion, is one of the three best new mags on the market, that the current trend toward on-line career searches and recruitment almost rivals the growth of e-mail. Pretty heady stuff when you think about the incredible spread of e-mail in just the last few years.

Internet detractors say that even though companies want to keep the best employees, the Internet is going to accelerate job hopping. It's probably true. Good thing? Bad thing? You decide. Some are concerned that pay disparities, what companies offer versus what employees demand, will widen as a result of all the information being put out there. Probably true. But that's the new age of employment; it's not going to be like it was in the past when management favored the old mushroom policy of keeping employees ignorant and in the dark, buried under several layers of manure. That's actually great for mushrooms, but not so great for employees.

Your career coach sees on-line career advancement as a very positive trend. My advice to the candidate and the company is to get involved in the job-seeking process. Learn it. Learn how it can be of benefit. Have fun with it. We live in a very exciting, dynamic world; the Internet is a big part of that world.

A client by the name of Mark Jordan came to me recently after hearing my radio show. His problem was that his wife had recently graduated from law school and had received an incredible job offer in the Seattle area (this is a problem?). They had decided to go, and Mark had also decided that after some years of being a civil engineer, he wanted to do something a little more challenging and exciting. So we put together a strategy to search via the Net in the Seattle area to see what was available. He'd check the hot companies, the job availability, the compensation packages, and so forth. What we finally did was post a job proposal (I know you remember the job proposal), on several job boards, in which he created a position for himself called the Chief Knowledge Officer (the CKO . . . Like it?) to be utilized by a big engineering firm that did structural as well as civil engineering. He would help drive them into the twenty-first century. And, as luck (or design) would have it, he was contacted by an engineering firm who liked the idea and they ended up negotiating a deal. Just another example of what you can accomplish by being creative and using the tools that are available.

Chapter Fourteen: Exercises

Internet Strategy and More

EXERCISE 1 Using the Internet

1. Schedule three or four hours to check out the top ten job posting sites on the Web (see page 219 for URLs). See what services they offer, and try a couple of searches in your industry in your area. You'll find some of the same listings on all the sites, but every site has a particular flavor. Register your profile on your two favorite sites. Ask for e-mail updates of likely jobs. See what kinds of inquiries that generates over the following month.

2. **Update your résumé.** I know, I know, we've been telling you over and over that résumés aren't the way to get jobs in the emerging economy, but they're still coin of the realm in Internet recruiting. When in Rome . . .

If you want to get hits from posting your résumé on-line, make sure you design a "keyword" résumé, which makes it easy for recruiters to search for key skills and job titles. Almost every job board has a page or two about how to write an effective on-line résumé. Read it, and follow its directions.

EXERCISE 2 The Passive Job Hunt Plan

Our advice is simple. In an economy that changes in the blink of an eye, and sometimes faster than that, you need to be ready to shift career gears equally quickly. That means passive job hunting needs to be a regular activity.

If I had only one word of advice about passive (and, for that matter, active) job hunting, it would be this:

Diversify!

You have no idea where the lead will come from which will land you your next job. Might be from your current employer. Might be from an on-line résumé posting. Might be from a casual conversation with your mechanic or your neighbor. Successful job hunting requires that you fish in more than one pond.

Unfortunately, most of us have been fishing in only one or two ponds. Most of my clients say that their entire job-hunting strategy has been sending resumes in response to newspaper ads. That's it. They never actually talk to anyone, unless they're lucky enough to get an interview. It's not long before the failure of this "strategy" to generate responses leads to frustration, disappointment, and a feeling of powerlessness. Rather than see this as a result of poor job-hunting strategy, most people take their lack of success as a reflection on their value. "I'm so worthless, no one wants to hire me." By the time (usually months later) they actually get a job offer, they're so amazed that someone wants to hire them that they'll take anything, even if it doesn't fit their career goals at all. And then, when they inevitably find themselves bored and frustrated in their new job, they refuse to go out and look again, because it was such a painful experience last time. Career Malaise 101.

Here's the really, really, really good news: **It doesn't have to be this way.**

EXERCISE 3 How to Diversify Your Job Hunting Strategy

1. **Decide how many hours per week you plan to spend on your passive job hunt.** I suggest no less than two hours. Four is ideal. If you're not working and involved in an active job hunt, consider it a full-time job, and schedule accordingly.

2. **Formulate a strategy** which includes at least *four* distinct elements. *Every* strategy should include networking.[1] You can select elements from the following list, if you find it helpful.

Networking	Newspaper ads
Informational interviewing	Researching companies
Professional groups	Job fairs
Internal searches (within your current company)	Researching industry trends
Internet postings	Recruiters and headhunters

3. **Prioritize your strategic elements.** Which is the most important? Which gives the most value for the time you invest? Which will be fun and rewarding enough that you'll actually do it?

4. **Make a pie chart.** Based on the relative importance of each element of your strategy, assign a certain amount of your time to it.

[1] Once you know what you want, you have to (HAVE TO!) tell people about it. Open your mouth, and talk to people. Lots of people. Go anywhere where there are people, and tell them who you are, what you want, and how they can help you. The more people you talk to, the more likely you are to fill your pipeline with leads.

Examples:

> *Senior management / executive level*
> Networking 50 percent
> Research 20 percent
> Internet 20 percent
> Headhunters/recruiters 10 percent
>
> *Entry-level sales*
> Research 30 percent
> Networking 20 percent
> Newspaper 25 percent
> Informational Interviewing 25 percent

COACH'S HINT: *A plan is only as good as the action you take on it. Plan your work, then work your plan.*

Time Management Tip:
Finding Time for the Passive Job Hunt

The Internet is without doubt a powerful tool for the career-minded individual like you. You can research, evaluate the market, see job postings, link with recruiters—a thousand things that can genuinely help you advance your career.

In my experience as a career coach, it's not lack of knowledge of these kinds of tools that sabotages people. It's not even technical expertise: the jobhunters' Internet is pretty user-friendly, and getting more so all the time.

More than any other factor, what prevents people from using the Internet is poor time management. If I can borrow an analogy from a friend of mine who's a personal trainer, even the fanciest treadmill won't get you fit unless you use it regularly. And the Internet won't help your career unless you find the time to use it.

So here's a simple time management principle which has proved to be very useful to ordinary busy people like you and me who can't seem to make time for passive job hunting.

Every day, spend time on your past, your present, and your future.

Work on the past can look like finishing up filing, answering last week's e-mails or yesterday's phone messages. The present is self-explanatory: doing the job that's right in front of you, meeting your commitments. The future segment is the time you commit to passive job hunting, networking, investing in productive relationships, building your star performer profile.

It's a little like a classic plan for how to spend your money: From every paycheck, put some toward paying off debt (past), some for current expenses and needs (present), and put some into investments and savings (future). If you ignore past and future in your financial life, get ready for trouble: Eventually (and it may not be for a while) your debt or lack of retirement savings will sabotage the present.

It's pretty clear that when you stand still in today's job market, you're actually going backward. Think of passive job hunting as investing part of your time in your future career success, just as you invest money in your 401K to ensure your future financial security.

Jobs of the Future

Call it what you will, but what's happening in the workplace—the combination of technology and the Internet—is nothing short of a revolution. I can't think of a single significant change in the United States over the past fifty years that has had the impact the Internet has. Typically, it took decades for changes of any kind to have an impact. And when they did, the effects sort of crept up on us. Cars, for example, dramatically changed our lives in the long run, but it actually took years before they were an accepted (and acceptable) part of our culture, and only gradually did they have an impact on how we did business. In only a few short years, though, the Internet has made huge inroads in the way we do business, and is soon expected to be a third of our gross national product.

There are some wonderful things that will be made possible

through all these changes. The job market has never been better (and will continue that way). Why? Because Alan Greenspan will keep the economy percolating along, and our labor shortage will continue until 2008, according to Harry Dent, Jr. It has never afforded better opportunities than it does now, not just in finding jobs, but in re-creating and reinventing the way we work on a daily basis. It's a privilege that's never been available. Before, our work was always well defined; we got a position description, a set of responsibilities, we came in every day, got our marching orders, and did basically the same thing we did the day before. But, corporate America has discovered it has to be flexible and able to change directions quickly, and the workforce has to be able to do the same. That's a good thing, it means more (and better) opportunities.

I understand that it's also a little scary for some of us who are not overly fond of change. For those of you who are just holding on till retirement, or don't want to do anything drastic because this week for sure you'll hit the Lotto, there'll probably always be some kind of position available. I don't imagine it will be anything terribly satisfying, but maybe you don't care. Just understand that there's a risk in staying where you are, and no guarantees just because you think you're holding on tighter than most. Guaranteed employment (the cradle-to-grave type) is a thing of the past. You're not going to work at the plant for forty years and then settle into a rocking chair. But if you continue to cultivate the soft skills we talked about, and strive to be a change agent, you're going to do exceptionally well in the workplace of tomorrow (which is actually already here).

You also want to be in partnership with your company. Rather than being employed *by*, you'll join *with*. Company success should be your success. By the same token, company failure might be our failure. Remember how I urged you to put skin in the game? This is what I meant: *We* deliver services. *We* create products. You want to be with a company that sees you as a partner rather than an employee.

Thousands of new jobs will be created as a result of the revolution, but technology and the Internet have done a lot more than just create jobs. Because of them, companies have had to reinvent their organizational structures.

Here are some examples of jobs that only exist because of the revolution we've been talking about. You may never have heard of them, but you could be perfect for them! These are from a magazine called *Business2.0*:

1. **New Metrics Analysts:** This person studies Internet traffic, how many people come on an Internet site. Sometimes these are called "hits," but the most appropriate designation is probably "unique visits." The New Metrics Analyst tracks the visits, analyzes the information, and determines how it affects your Internet business. They track frequency of visits, the length of visits; they detect patterns, and they make recommendations based on what they find. What skills would you need to do this job well? You should have an ability to perform quantitative analysis, have database experience, and know how to translate that data into useful information. The salary range currently is from 60 to 110K.

2. **Virtual Organization Leader:** Here, the employee moves from project to project with the employer assembling a team of experts needed to complete a particular assignment. When it's completed, the VOL disassembles that team and moves on to the next project. Candidates for this job must understand how business goal strategies interrelate with the resources that are available, and how to use those resources to achieve specific goals. They must have good leadership and people skills, and have the ability to work under a tight schedule. The salary range is from 60 to 90K.

3. **Content Engineer:** This man or woman acts as a liaison between the information technology group, the marketing group, and the suppliers. He/she gathers information, figures out what content fits into the company's overall business objectives, and makes determinations about what to use and when to use the applicable content. A Content Engineer should have some

technical background, but mainly understand who the audience is, what's important, what's not, what's trivial, and what's vital. Salary range is from 50 to 80K.

4. **Chief Community Strategist:** The big trend today is toward community-based Web sites, a series of departments or communities that together present a one-stop source for information on a particular subject. A great example of this is *iVillage.com*, a women's issues Web site with something like fifteen to twenty departments, chat rooms, bulletin boards, and guest speakers. The Chief Community Strategist serves as a direct link between the Web site members (people who sign up to visit the site regularly) and the company top executives. They develop reports based on feedback they get from various sources within the community Web site (e-mail, bulletin boards, chat rooms). The company uses that information to come up with new ideas and new features. You should have some operations experience, some management experience, but the most important thing is understanding how the community interacts within itself and how all that relates to the company. Expect to be paid between 120 to 150K.

5. **Ethical Hacker:** I just love this title. It seems to carry the meaning of oxymoron to new heights. The hacker, who has always had the bad reputation of being someone who tries to break in to a legitimate enterprise, is now being paid to do what is essentially authorized espionage. You'll need an expertise in multiple operating systems, software applications, security software, and networking protocols, and in-depth knowledge of the computer itself and how to navigate. In other words, you have to be a great hacker. But some companies take this very seriously, proven by the fact that they're willing to pay 60 to 140K for these skills.

6. **E-mail Channel Specialist:** Some Web site businesses believe that e-mail is the next great channel for products and services and direct marketing. This person defines policy and

strategic plans relating to how to use it (e-mail), delivers information to top management, and oversees the testing of new products to see how they fit into the overall business strategy. Skills needed: software development skills, people skills, and an ability to understand trends and numbers. The salary range is currently 95 to 180K, proof that e-mail is huge and it's only going to get bigger.

7. **Consumer Experience Manager:** This position might have been called Operations Manager at one time—the person who works with purchasing and distribution and makes strategic decisions. Instead of the former *re*active way of dealing almost exclusively with customer complaints, companies now have more of a *pro*active position that wants not only to solve problems, but to actually improve the entire consumer experience. This person works with the content team and the application developers and comes up with new features and functions that make the shopping experience better. Skills needed: operations experience, strategic planning skills, and, of course, people skills. The salary range is 125 to 150K.

8. **Metamediary CEO:** This key figure is the liaison between the buyers and sellers of an Internet-based business, and works closely with third party or strategic partners. He also takes a global look at enhancing Web site content and features. Skills needed: great negotiating skills, great business acumen, an understanding of product and marketing, and how to help conceive new features and services for a company Web site. The salary is about 250K. Keep in mind that while a very important position, this is not the company CEO in charge of overall operations.

9. **Chief Knowledge Officer:** This is something of a regeneration of the CIO (Chief Information Officer) that came into play about ten years ago, the person who ran the computer department within a company. The CKO is responsible for building and maintaining the company's internal knowl-

edge management efforts, meaning how learning happens within the company, and how all this newly developed "knowledge capital" is shared among all employees. She is also responsible for the databases, programs, documents, and people who are involved in the effort. In addition, she might provide education for internal and external customers to teach them how to use the system. This is a position that's a much more comprehensive and expanded version of the old CIO. Someone with lots of technical background, the ability to adapt methodologies to specific tasks, and a deep understanding of how individuals work together. The salary range is 100 to 500K.

10. **Chief Internet Officer:** Here, the employee runs the company Internet, particularly from a technological standpoint. Where the Knowledge Officer pulls a lot of different pieces of the company's Internet information together, the Internet Officer is primarily responsible for the Internet site itself. He needs to know management practices, have a fundamental understanding of the economics of business, and have a strong technical background. The pay is good, between 200 to 300K.

Those are just a few of the new positions available today. Now, you may not want any of the ten jobs listed above, but the emerging company is going to allow (encourage) people (you . . . yes, you) to come forward with these kinds of ideas and they're going to pay you handsomely for the privilege of using them.

I guarantee you that more are being developed, since we have just begun to scratch the surface of what's possible in the Internet Age. As you can see, you don't have to be a technical whiz or someone who can write code in four different languages to do well in the workplace of tomorrow. But you will get farther faster if you have the ability to navigate through the Net. Bottom line is that the pioneers who are coming up with new ideas for their company are being given unprecedented pay, unprecedented flexibility, and are having a real impact on what happens in the workplace. They're developing concepts and coming up with ways to launch new and better ways to do business. They're making a difference. They're being change agents.

You think the guy who came up with the idea of hiring an Ethical Hacker was some kind of a techno-whiz-nerd? My guess is that he (or she) wasn't. They probably were somebody who thought of the obvious: If we want to hacker-proof our system, why don't we hire someone who's successfully broken into it? Makes sense. You want to burglar-proof your home, you ought to consult with a successful (ex) burglar.

Someone wanted to be serious about customer satisfaction and decided that they'd deal with the problem before they got to the complaint stage. Enter the Consumer Experience Manager.

We're not talking about learning the Theory of Relativity here. You don't have to be a budding Einstein to come up with some viable concepts that will help your business. Don't leave it to them (whoever "them" is—or are—in your company). Get used to the idea that you're "them." It's *your* company.

Is there a conclusion in all of this? Is there something you can take away and keep in mind regarding your career management plan going forward? You bet there is. Grab onto **THE RULES HAVE CHANGED.** It's vital that you understand that. For the most part, the changes are very positive. But whether you think of them as positive or not, get used to the idea. Remember that change not only creates opportunities, it multiplies them. They're outsourcing what you do at work? Good. Become an independent contractor and bid on the contract. Who better than you? Nobody, that's who.

Some of today's jobs will vanish. The people who made buggy whips probably ended up making upholstery for car seats. Or making engine parts. Though there was fear that nothing would take a buggy whip's place, in fact, there were *more* jobs available after their demise. Turns out there were a lot more cars than buggies.

But many of us will be doing things we'd never imagined we could do. In five years, projections are that 50 percent of the jobs will be technology based and 50 percent of us will work for technology-based companies. Doesn't mean we'll all have to be techno whizzes. Companies still need accountants and support people of all kinds.

I wish we could come up with a different word for work, because I think what we'll be doing in the future is different. "Work" carries all the old connotations of nose-to-the-grindstone, tough-job, sweat, drudgery, and in general something unpleasant.

I'm a perfect example. I served my time in corporate America, had some good experiences, some not so good experiences. I eventually became a free agent and got to create a whole new set of responsibilities that were more in line with what I wanted to do. Sure, I took a chance, but doesn't any real worthwhile venture require a little risk?

So research, read, and go for it. Above all, enjoy the journey... because it's all a journey. There really is no top of the mountain, no perfect pinnacle, so you might as well stop worrying about whether you're going to get there. What you do have are choices. You can struggle up the mountain and tell yourself it'll all be better when you get to the top, thus setting yourself up for disappointment. Or you can have a good time, enjoy all the beautiful scenery, and realize that there's really no top to get to, because the journey never ends.

Good luck and **go confidently in the direction of your dream!**

Chapter Fifteen: Exercises

EXERCISE 1
Are You Ready for the Revolution?

Emotional Intelligence in the New Workplace

The new workplace has opportunities galore. But there's one final and fundamental trait you need to develop for the new workplace. We'll shamelessly borrow Daniel Goleman's term, and call it emotional intelligence, or EQ.

A star performer of the 1980s had drive, ambition, intensity, and tunnel vision about achieving his goals. It was a "me first" decade. Teamwork was irrelevant, competition dominated collaboration.

A star performer of the 1990s had a grasp of emerging technology, an understanding of diversity, a quick learning curve, and true adaptability. It was a "faster is better" decade. Many people found themselves playing a new game by the old rules.

In the new millennium, the profile of the star performer has changed again, and it includes a far higher level of emotional intelligence than ever before. Today's star performers have reached the point where they acknowledge the truth of the following elements.

- They recognize that security comes from adaptability, preparedness, and courage, not from the solid, safe job (these rare animals are now on the verge of extinction).

- They have a higher tolerance of risk in their career.

- They take full responsibility for their career, their performance, even their company's performance, knowing that no one else will do it for them.

- They have a deep commitment to ongoing learning and personal development.

- They have the ability to embrace change gracefully, making it an ally not an enemy.

- They routinely and rapidly shift their perspective, not only thinking outside of the box, but stepping away from the box altogether.

- They identify, work from, and constantly expand their core competencies.

- They know how to clear the detritus of the past, live flexibly in the present, and keep one eye firmly on the future.

- They practice nonattachment: If a project or idea doesn't work, they don't fight and scrap to save a sinking ship, they learn from it and let it go. (Winston Churchill is quoted as saying, "Success is moving rapidly from failure to failure without losing enthusiasm.")

- They do not confuse their career with their life.

All of the above criteria require this quality of emotional intelligence. I strongly recommend reading Daniel Goleman's excellent book *Emotional Intelligence* to find out more about EQ.

If you happen to have a high IQ, this can of course profoundly help your career, but it's no longer enough on its own. Many people with genius level IQs are not especially successful in the new workplace if, for example, they lack social skills and communication skills—the classic computer nerd.

It is becoming increasingly clear that the new workplace effectively selects for people with a high EQ. A high EQ implies the ability to respond and successfully adapt to *personal* challenges as well as the professional challenges that typically defined the territory of the workplace. It's another way of saying that soft skills and people skills count for more today than they ever have.

To summarize the above, increasing your chances of success in the new workplace requires a high EQ, and developing your EQ requires a commitment to personal development. I believe that this accounts for the birth of the coaching profession, the ever-expanding library of excellent books on aspects of personal development, and the availability of thousands upon thousands of workshops, trainings, and seminars on personal development topics. We've come a long way from the days when your only real avenue for personal development was several years of therapy. In the accelerated business climate of the twenty-first century, many people simply don't have time for that any more.

So how do you enhance your EQ? You develop a . . .

EXERCISE 2   Personal Development Plan

You now have literally thousands of possible choices for your personal development, and an understanding (we hope) of why it's important for your career. The next step is to make a plan. Here are some ways to do that:

1. Hire a coach.

I freely admit to being biased here. Coaching is the most potent, effective, and timely method to advance your personal development. It's individualized, focused, and fast. You can enter into the realm of personal development in the company of an experienced guide. With his help, you will go places you wouldn't go on your own, stretch your comfort zone, challenge yourself to really live up to your potential. It works, it's fun, and the effects can last forever.

2. Build a reading list of self-development books.
Commit to reading one book per month, and applying what it says.

3. Research classes, seminars, and workshops.
Choose some areas where you feel you need development, or where you want to take an existing competency to the next level. Make a training budget for yourself, and schedule at least one training per quarter.

4. Find a mentor.
Choose someone who can observe, evaluate, and contribute to your progress along your self-development path. It should be someone whom you admire and aspire to emulate.

Conclusion

If you've followed the exercises in this book, you should now be equipped with:

- A Career map that matches who you are and what you want
- An individual development plan to increase your EQ
- A greater understanding of the new economy
- A healthy dose of Internet savvy
- Some strategies for taming your critic
- A brand identity for the brand called you
- Strategies for getting big raises, fun projects, and new opportunities

CONGRATULATIONS!
YOU'RE READY FOR THE REVOLUTION.

Fastest-Growing Occupations (Overall)

Listed below are the twenty-five occupations projected to grow the fastest during the 1996–2006 time period.

OCCUPATION	EMPLOYMENT		PERCENT CHANGE
	1996	2006	
Computer engineers	215,700	451,000	109%
Systems analysts, electronic data processing	505,500	1,025,100	103%
Personal and home care aides	202,500	373,900	85%
Physical and corrective therapy assistants and aides	84,500	150,900	79%
Home health aides	494,700	872,900	77%
Electronic pagination system operators	30,400	52,800	74%
Medical assistants	224,800	391,200	74%
Physical therapists	114,500	195,600	71%
Occupational therapy assistants and aides	15,700	26,400	69%
Paralegal personnel	112,900	189,300	68%
Occupational therapists	57,400	95,300	66%
Teachers, special education	407,000	647,700	59%
Human services workers	177,800	276,300	55%
Data processing equipment repairers	79,700	121,500	52%
Medical records technicians	87,300	131,800	51%
Speech-language pathologists and audiologists	87,300	131,500	51%
Amusement and recreation attendants	288,100	426,100	48%
Dental hygienists	132,800	196,800	48%
Physician's assistants	63,800	93,500	47%
Adjustment clerks	401,300	583,900	46%
Respiratory therapists	81,800	119,300	46%
Emergency medical technicians	149,700	217,100	45%
Engineering, mathematical, and natural sciences managers	342,900	498,000	45%
Manicurists	43,100	62,400	45%

Index